SCOTLAND'S HERALDIC HERITAGE

THE LION REJOICING

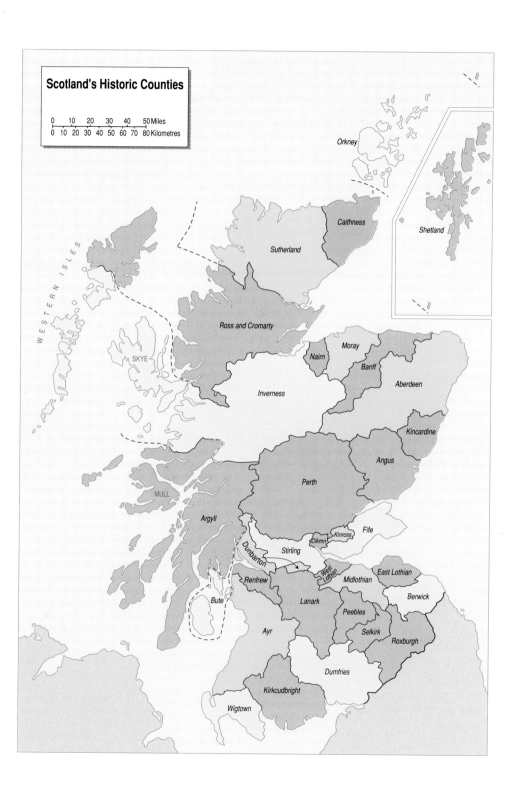

Scotland's Historic Counties

0   10   20   30   40   50 Miles
0 10 20 30 40 50 60 70 80 Kilometres

Orkney

Shetland

Caithness

Sutherland

WESTERN ISLES

SKYE

Ross and Cromarty

Moray

Nairn

Banff

Aberdeen

Inverness

Kincardine

Angus

MULL

Perth

Argyll

Fife

Kinross

Clkmn

Dunbarton

Stirling

West Lothian

East Lothian

Renfrew

Midlothian

Bute

Berwick

Lanark

Peebles

Selkirk

Ayr

Roxburgh

Dumfries

Kirkcudbright

Wigtown

CONTENTS

ACKNOWLEDGEMENTS

The authors are indebted to Sir Malcolm R Innes of Edingight, KCVO, The Rt Hon The Lord Lyon King of Arms, for granting permission to reproduce illustrations from sources in the Lyon Office, Edinburgh.

We also acknowledge permission from Mrs Fay Pottinger to publish examples of work executed by the late Don Pottinger, Islay Herald of Arms.

Especial thanks are given to Mr J White, Historic Scotland, and to Ms Gillian Kerr and her colleagues at The Stationery Office for their advice, assistance and encouragement, and to Tom Mason at Centre Graphics for his skilful page make-up.

Certain other individuals were also most helpful and we thank The Lord President of the Court of Session, The Minister of the High Kirk of St Giles, Mrs CGW Roads MVO, Lyon Clerk and Keeper of Records, Dr Patrick Barden, Mr A Carswell, Mrs J Edwards, Mr Leslie Hodgson, Mrs MJ McDonald, Mr W Wallace Jones and Romilly Squire Esq.

Finally to Mrs Lekky Shepherd, Series Editor of Discovering Historic Scotland, heartfelt gratitude is expressed for her patience, understanding, and skilful advice which have prevented the authors from issuing challenges on the field of tourney!

FOREWORD

Scotland is a country where the imprint of history is still clearly visible in the landscape, in its houses, churches, farmsteads and settlements large and small. All these have coloured, and been coloured by, their setting in mountains or moorland, on fertile pasture or sandy shore, at loch-side or rivermouth. Of paramount importance has always been the all-encompassing influence of the sea, for Scotland is set amidst the searoads of the Celtic provinces in the west and the Scandinavian regions to the north. The trading routes with the mainland of Europe to the east and the land and sea approaches to that dominant neighbour, England, in the south. Scotland's cultural history has thus been moulded by a mixture of influences, fluctuating in importance, absorbed and transformed in ways that are peculiarly Scottish. This series aims to provide a view across the mosaic of that history from its earliest beginnings to the present day. Each volume covers one individual aspect of the panorama but the themes are interwoven: kings and queens, heraldry and houses, wars and warriors, stained glass and churches – all link to create a tapestry of Scotland's vigorous past and her historic present.

Heraldry is a subject which is visible to most of us in ways of which we are scarcely aware. The rules that govern its continued existence – firmly adhered to and upheld with the weight of law – are described here in detail. The complex designs, each speaking, silently, the lineage of their holder, are miracles of compression, encoding information on family, status and history in brilliant form. This volume enables everyone to crack the code and read the symbols, at the same time marvelling at their colour and vibrancy and at their survival, speaking to us as much as any other historic artefact of past ages and lives.

ALEXANDRA SHEPHERD
Series Editor

tres hault et trespuissant v. du nom

tres excellent prince Jacques Roy d'escosse

In my defens

The original stall plate of the Scottish King having been lost, this replacement was gifted by The Heraldry Society of Scotland. A.D. 1982.

INTRODUCTION

OPPOSITE: *The lion rejoices today as an echo from the past. This is a modern replacement of the stallplate, now lost, which recorded the appointment of James V, King of Scots, as a Knight of the Burgundian Order of the Golden Fleece. The panel, rich in colour and glowing with gold leaf, hangs within Tournai Cathedral, Belgium (Burnett).*

Heraldry is the fusion of fact and fancy, myth and manner, romance and reality. It is an exuberant union of family, art and history. In this realm of infinite imagination and fine point of law the unicorn still roams unremarked, the spike-snouted tyger disports with his zoological Bengal cousin, and the basilisk passes unnoticed. It is the enduring, triumphal marriage of Man and Symbol.

Some of Scotland's earliest heraldic symbols? Serpent, 'double-disc and Z rod' and the mirror and comb adorn a 6th-7th-century AD Pictish stone at Aberlemno, Angus. Their meaning is uncertain but each symbol may identify a tribal or family group (Burnett).

Human beings have at all times dared to identify with powers felt but unseen around them and, in symbols, have systematically attempted to draw and bind those unseen powers to them. We give them signs that we may invoke and understand them. We then adopt and wear those signs that we may acquire the identity, strength, virtue or protection they may afford us. We are the only creatures to use symbols, and we use them lavishly. Be it religious, political, occupational, traffic, or trademark, we are every day surrounded with a web of cultural imagery, a wide ranging vocabulary of shared, immediately recognisable signs and **symbols**.

One detailed system of symbols, the laws and usage of coats of arms and their accessories, is called **armory**, the science of heraldry. It is a system developed from a medieval knightly totemism, the identification of family and fief with certain symbols passed

down from generation to generation, or passing on to the successor lords of a territory. The system burst forth almost complete at its inception as part of the great cultural expansion of the 12th century and the triumph of the feudal system across Europe.

In its simplest form, **heraldry** is the custom of identifying one warrior by a device or symbol, his **arms**, painted on his shield, his banner, and often on his tunic – his coat of arms. Of itself, this was not new; what distinguished the developing practice as heraldry was the rise by the end of the 12th century of a common European system of conventions and symbols and the fact these designs were inherited. As they were heritable they had also to be shared out between a knight's sons or passed through his daughters, and regular systems of *differencing* the basic arms were devised so each son might be seen to be both his father's son and his own man. With the spread of armory there arose in the 13th century a small corps of men disciplined in the new science and entrusted with its recording and control. These were, and are, the **Officers of Arms**, commonly called **heralds** but ranked from earliest times from *pursuivant* through *herald* to *king of arms*, sometimes retained by one lord, sometimes freelance, and occasionally organised into guilds or colleges. So complete was their mastery that the art took its other name from them – heraldry.

The famous arms of the Latin Kingdom of Jerusalem founded by the successful First Crusade: Argent a cross potent between four crosslets Or. Like the arms of the Papal See, it violates the basic rule prohibiting placing gold on silver as a means of stressing their peculiar significance (Burnett).

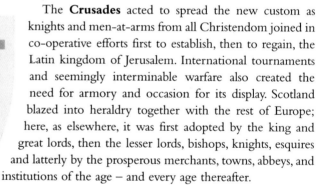

The **Crusades** acted to spread the new custom as knights and men-at-arms from all Christendom joined in co-operative efforts first to establish, then to regain, the Latin kingdom of Jerusalem. International tournaments and seemingly interminable warfare also created the need for armory and occasion for its display. Scotland blazed into heraldry together with the rest of Europe; here, as elsewhere, it was first adopted by the king and great lords, then the lesser lords, bishops, knights, esquires and latterly by the prosperous merchants, towns, abbeys, and institutions of the age – and every age thereafter.

The major part of Europe is essentially at peace now and with a greater degree of conceptual unity than might have been thought possible since it was simply Christendom. The Crusades are history. No one now dons his crested helm, raises up his banner, hoists his shield and rides to battle or in the tourney. But never have the Scots heralds been busier. Armory flourishes here as never before: perhaps this is because it can still be seen as a celebration of Scotland, her land, her institutions and above all, her people. It is a brave and joyous tradition stretching back 800 years which yet remains as fresh and vital as tomorrow's next grant of arms.

THE ORIGINS OF ARMORY

The precise origins of armory are as conjectural as those of football. Doubtless there were similar ball games prior to football's coalescence as a sport with uniformly observed rules and standards. Likewise there had always been some usage for identifying members of a host in battle. Like football, too, the benefit of a fixed system of international rules was immediately recognised and quickly replaced the earlier informal practices. Thus the medieval lord's badge and livery colours made his following instantly identifiable to one another and all others. It was the feudal strip. The military unit in the Middle Ages did not comprise vast regiments or divisions but was formed of the lord's own vassals, friends, neighbours and relatives: in an age of uncertain alliances, **allegiance** was to one's lord before the Crown. The men were as proud of their distinctive emblems and colours, their lord's badges and liveries, as he was – vanity must have played as much a role as military identification – and were as ready to display them as a team's supporters are today.

HERALDRY IN SCOTLAND

The earliest examples of armorial usage which survive in Scotland are the **seal impressions** on charters of Alan and his son, Walter, successively High Stewards of Scotland from 1177 to 1241. The seals show the *fess chequy* of the Stewarts, still such a common feature of Scots heraldry. Similarly, a seal of Patrick Dunbar, 5th Earl of Dunbar (1182–1232) displays him armed and mounted with a lion rampant on his shield, a device still carried by the Dunbars. Indeed, before 1250 there is evidence that most of the great families had already settled on the emblems, or cognisances, by which they are recognised today; for example, the lions of Galloway, Angus, and Wallace; the escallops of Graham; the escutcheons (shields) of Hay; crescents of Seton; garbs (sheaves) of Comyn; and saltire and chief of the Bruces, all of which may be seen every day seven and a half centuries later.

The character of Scotland's people has given heraldry a special place in the cultural life of this ancient realm. For the Scot, heraldry can show **ancestry**, provide historical fact and express national **identity**. It can provide proof of **ownership** on the one hand and be used to display personal beliefs on the other. In a less wealthy country, the former reason is important.

The 'feudal strip' (Dennis).

Privy seal used c. 1200 by Walter, son of Alan, both High Stewards of Scotland. It shows the fess chequy still borne by the many Stewart branches today.

11

Personal silver engraved with the arms of Grizel Baillie of Jarviswood (Burnett).

Valuable items of gold and silver can be made personal by marking them with the unique set of heraldic symbols allocated to an individual. Crested silver is an obvious example, but any precious personal item can be identified by heraldry. Valuable objects were often handed down through several generations and could be marked with the differing arms of each owner, and illustrated here are a silver coffee pot and jug, examples of this practice.

The fabulous crest of the Earl of Hopetoun, the ephemeral made solid (Fairbairn).

Scotland was never on a par with England or continental countries in terms of wealth, so that excessive display has seldom been a feature of Scottish culture. Those members of the community who could afford some extra decoration on buildings or personal possessions proclaimed ownership by means of armorial ensigns. These in turn provided ornament and so combined **status** and **decoration** as one – a practical solution which appealed to the careful nature of the canny Scot! Between 1400 and 1700 it can be argued that heraldry was the dominant decorative motif found in Scotland.

Scotland's artistic reputation does not compare with that of ancient Greece or late medieval Italy, but by the middle of the 17th century a distinctly Scottish style of

The defaced Arms of the Earl of Gowrie

If possession and display of arms indicate status and rank, the loss of one can result in the loss of the other. One man who conspired against James VI, King of Scots, John, Earl of Gowrie, was found guilty of treason in 1600 and a public ceremony was performed to expunge the name and Arms of Gowrie. He became non-heraldic when a painting of his arms was torn in half and hung upside down on the Mercat Cross in Edinburgh. Illustrated here is a page from the armorial record book of Lyon Sir Robert Foreman of Luthrie showing the cancellation of the Gowrie coat of arms from the heraldic records of Scotland (Lyon Office).

architecture and design had evolved with characteristic features. These did not lack artistic imagination, and heraldry formed an integral part of the vernacular vocabulary. The style evolved as a result of climate, materials available, outside influence, social conditions and limited means.

The continuous use of heraldry over some 800 years in Scotland reflects changing cultural attitudes and artistic styles. Medieval heraldry was simple and effective for battlefield use. Later peaceful periods saw armorial designs become more elaborate where instant recognition at a distance was no longer a priority. *Paper* heraldry was the fashion, artistic flights of fantasy drawn on a flat surface without thought of practical use. Crests which were once modelled in three dimensions and fixed to knightly helmets became only possible on paper. The crest of the Earl of Hopetoun (opposite), for example, incorporates an ephemeral rainbow and clouds.

During the 19th century heraldic art went through a decline.

Armorial achievement of Admiral Viscount Duncan of Camperdown which incorporates the gold medal awarded after his great naval victory. This is typical of late 18th- and early 19th-century style (Burnett).

Shields were enlarged, helmets became very small, and mantling was so convoluted it looked like seaweed. Symbolism on a shield was replaced with pictorial imagery, resulting in, for example, a very

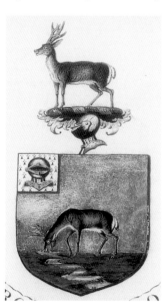

The pictorial arms of the Scottish painter, Sir Henry Raeburn. An example of canting, or punning arms, this refers to Psalm 42: 'Like as the hart desireth the water-brook', in presenting a 'roe' [deer] at a 'burn'. The motto 'Robur in Deo' is another play on the name (Lyon Office).

inartistic coat of arms for Scotland's leading portrait painter, Sir Henry Raeburn. Many famous sailors and soldiers who achieved prominence in the Napoleonic Wars recorded their exploits for posterity by placing scenes of, or the rewards from, their triumphs on their coats of arms. Admiral Lord Duncan utilised the gold medal awarded for his sea victory at Camperdown; Colonel John Cameron of Fashiefern captured the French town of Aire and this is reproduced on his shield.

Current heraldic practice in Scotland has reverted to the old simplicity and proportions of

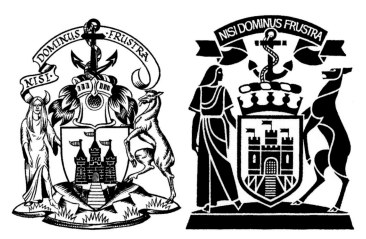

A pictorial rendering of the arms of the City of Edinburgh (Mitchell); and, right, the stylised version of the same arms (Pottinger) to illustrate variation of style.

medieval armory, a style which is in harmony with modern graphic design. One artist who led in this revival was the late J I D Pottinger, Islay Herald and Lyon Clerk (1919–1986). Illustrations of the 'old' and 'new' arms for the former City of Edinburgh District Council demonstrate how Pottinger translated one Scottish achievement to suit modern graphic requirements. His book, *Simple Heraldry,* was a major contribution to the understanding and enjoyment of heraldry by a wider public. We hope our volume may continue in that tradition.

To that end our approach is in two parts. In the first two chapters we describe the history and science of armory, the rules governing it and how they were, and are, applied. In the subsequent chapters we look in detail at heraldry in action, first in the royal arms then through the wider architectural and material culture of the land. Throughout we hope to highlight the theme of the continued use and adaptation of an ancient and colourful art.

The Armes of Sr Dauid Lindesay of the mont
Knyght. Alias lion Kuŋ of armes auter of
this put buke. Anno dm 1542

Cavitas
Cavitas
Cavitas
fides
Spes

IAVME

CHAPTER 1

THE GENTLE SCIENCE

OPPOSITE: *Achievement of Sir David Lindsay of the Mount, Lyon King of Arms, from his own armorial or book of arms, the earliest officially recognised Register of Arms in Scotland. Lindsay was a renaissance man, indeed combining his duties as Lyon with statesmanship, poetry and play writing under James V.*

Armory is one of those happy fields where art and system combine. Perhaps daunting at first glance, it resolves itself quickly into a comprehensible and entertaining study and a delightful introduction to the history of Scotland and her families.

The **laws of heraldry** were developed by the early 14th century and are generally observed, with only minor variations, throughout Europe and those countries with a European tradition. The systematic exposition of the rules and usages of heraldry in Scotland was first undertaken in 1680 by the stalwart King's Advocate, Sir George Mackenzie of Rosehaugh, known to the Covenanters as 'Bluidy Mackenzie' . His work, *The Science of Herauldry treated as part of the Civil Law and Law of Nations...*[etc.], still accepted today as legal authority, is part of the great flowering of Scottish legal literature of that age. Mackenzie was followed by Alexander Nisbet, whose authoritative *System of Heraldry* was first published in 1722. We can do no better than to quote from Nisbet's preface:

Portrait engraving from the frontispiece of The Science of Herauldry... *&t of its author, Sir George Mackenzie of Rosehaugh.*

> *As Heraldry itself is of a noble extract and original, so the knowledge thereof is worthy of any gentleman: and, if duly considered, will be found no less useful than curious; as tending to illustrate the histories not only of particular families, but of the nation in general.*
>
> *The original design of heraldry is not merely show and pageantry, as some are apt to imagine, but to distinguish persons and families; to represent the heroic achievements of our*

Engraving of a carved stone panel from the wall of the house of Alexander Nisbet's grandfather and displaying his arms: Argent three boars heads erased Sable. It is perhaps fitting that no portrait, only the arms, survive of Scotland's greatest armorist.

ancestors, and to perpetuate their memory; to trace the origin of noble and ancient families, and the various steps by which they arrived at greatness; to distinguish the many different branches descended from the same families, and to show the several relations which one family stands in to another.

The recognition and composition of arms and their arrangement or marshalling is the gentle science of armory. There are a few rules which will make most heraldry easily intelligible and help the observer to discriminate between the genuine and the bogus.

THE RULES OF ARMORY

The first rule of armory is: **One man / One Coat of Arms**. This is simple and fundamental – and much too often ignored. It is no accident that the rise of armory parallels the practice of using surnames in northern Europe – likewise fixed and heritable. Heraldry is essentially identification. There is no more sense in such a solecism as a single 'Smith Family Coat of Arms', or, even more misleading, the 'Smith Crest', than there would be in giving all Smiths the identical forenames in addition to their shared surname. Certainly, arms within the extended family will share common elements, but they equally must proclaim their individual identities.

In Scotland the rule is also the **law**, unlike the situation in England where there exists no penal jurisdiction to enforce the law of arms. There the somewhat lax practice is to grant arms then allow the various scions of the family to add their own marks of difference; and there is nothing to prevent the selling of representations of 'family arms', or even more disingenuously 'arms for your surname', on the basis of a shared or similar name, without *differencing* or even determining the slightest degree of actual relationship. This is quite illegal in Scotland where each branch of the family will matriculate its properly differenced version of the arms of the head of the family through the Lyon Office and where the Procurator Fiscal of the Lyon Court has statutory authority to prosecute any fraud.

A naked warning to any who might attempt to usurp the coat of arms of a Scot, from the charming Simple Heraldry, Cheerfully Illustrated *of the late Sir Iain Moncrieffe of that Ilk, Bt, later Albany Herald, and the late Don Pottinger, later Lyon Clerk and Islay Herald.*

The blazon

Blazon is the **key** to armory. It is both the noun and verb to describe the elements of a coat of arms. Arms are recorded, transmitted, and depicted by blazon. In the clear words of Sir Thomas Innes of Learney (Lord Lyon 1945–69):

> *To blazon a coat of arms is to describe it scientifically, in words which cannot be misunderstood, just as a doctor writes a prescription, or an architect a specification. From a correct blazon, anyone versed in heraldry can instantly picture what the arms look like, and draw a reproduction of a shield he has never seen.*

The second fundamental rule of armory is that the design must be able to be reduced to an **intelligible blazon** – a written conventional formula – which can be understood and the arms recreated by any herald anywhere. The language is archaic French and admittedly obscure, but its ancient continuity requires it be respected and preserved. Thus the blazon 'Argent three escutcheons Gules', at first sight mere gibberish, will always and everywhere be immediately recognised by any armorist as a white shield with three small red shields on it, arranged as two over one – the ancient and present arms of the Earl of Erroll, Chief of the Hays. This is the simple and enduring language of heraldry.

The colours of heraldry

The **tinctures** of armory are ordered into five 'colours', two 'metals' and three 'stains'. The traditional five colours are: *Gules* (red), *Azure* (blue), *Vert* (green), *Sable* (black), and *Purpure* (purple). These may be depicted in any shade as long as it is the correct hue: thus Gules may be anything from scarlet to deep crimson, and Azure may run from navy to pale blue where appropriate, though a middle tone is usual. There are three **stains** sometimes met with: a mulberry or maroon (*Murrey*), a tawny orange (*Tenné*), and an indefinite reddish blood colour (*Sanguine*). These constitute the conventional colours of heraldry. However, anything may be depicted in its natural colours. It is then blazoned as *proper*. Thus a brown dog would have to be blazoned 'a brown dog proper', while a black one would be 'a dog Sable'.

Offsetting the colours are the two **metals** of armory, *Or* and *Argent*. Or is literally gold and may be depicted as gilt, though commonly painted as a shade of yellow or ochre. Argent (silver) may likewise be silvered or painted a pale grey, but usually it is simply white. It is the most common field for Scottish arms.

The third rule of armory is the famous injunction that **colour may never be placed on colour** nor metal on metal. It is a necessary practice to ensure **visibility**; a Sable figure on a shield Vert will be indistinguishable at any distance. Were it on Argent it would be very clear. Of course there are exceptions – including the blanket exception for anything proper – but the rule is a good one and carefully followed.

An heraldic tree of metals, colours and stains. When making line drawings of arms a system of 'tricking' or abbreviation is employed using the first two or three letters of the colour, thus: Ar, Gu, Az, Sa, Vt and Pur, to indicate the colouration (Dennis). RIGHT: *the points and parts of a shield.*

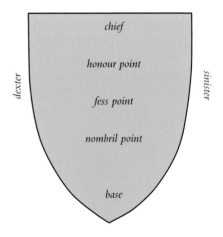

chief

honour point

dexter

fess point

sinister

nombril point

base

Ermine   Contre-ermine   Vair   Contre-vair

Erminois

Vairy
Or and
Sable

Pean   Potent

The furs

The availability of the heraldic **furs**, which are neither colour nor metal, help to observe the rule and provide variety. These take the form of certain conventional all-over patterns derived from actual furs. *Ermine* is white or silver with black tail spots. *Contre-ermine* is black with white spots, and there are other rare variations. *Vair* is a cheery pattern of blue and white squirrel skins. It can be depicted in other colour/metal combinations if specified in the blazon and in different patterns as shown in the illustration. Heraldic furs are never painted on a shield to give the impression of actual fur.

The formula of a blazon always begins by describing the **field** of the shield, which will be one of these metals, tinctures, furs, or, rarely, stains. After the field comes the principal ordinary, if any, then charges. Lastly a chief or bordure, if there is one, and anything placed 'over all' (explained further below).

The shield is divided as shown into **points** and **parts** (opposite). The *dexter* is the right side of a shield as carried, not as seen. The *sinister* is the left. As a basic rule in heraldry, the dexter and chief, or top part, are more 'honourable' than the sinister or the base.

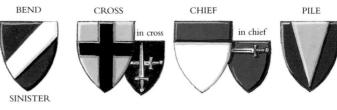

BEND   CROSS   CHIEF   PILE

in cross   in chief

SINISTER

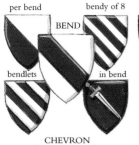

per bend   bendy of 8

BEND

bendlets   in bend

CHEVRON

chevronels   per chevron

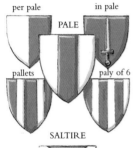

per pale   in pale

PALE

pallets   paly of 6

SALTIRE

per saltire   in saltire

tierced in pairle   PALL   tierced in pairle reversed

pall couped or shakefork

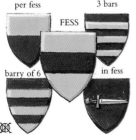

per fess   3 bars

FESS

barry of 6   in fess

The shapes of heraldry – ordinaries and subordinaries

Ordinaries are conventional, bold geometric figures placed on a shield. They may have been derived from structural bands strengthening the shield. Armorists differ as to a definitive list, but generally they are the broad bands: vertical or *pale*, horizontal or *fess*, diagonals or *bend* and *bend sinister*, and the top band of the shield or *chief*. Then there are the cross and especially the 'X'-shaped *saltire*, the cross of St Andrew, such a common feature of Scots heraldry. Lastly there are the narrow 'V' or *pile*, the broad inverted 'V' of the *chevron* and the 'Y'-shaped *pall*. Curiously, heraldic practice makes no provision for any curved ordinary.

As a general rule of practice, there will only be one ordinary on a shield, though a chief is frequently combined with the others. When more than one is borne, it will be reduced in size and called by its diminutive name. Thus, two fesses become *bars*, pales become *pallets* and chevrons are *chevronels*. The **diminutives** may sometimes be reduced further. A bend is reduced to a *bendlet* which is further narrowed to a *riband*. A riband in bend sinister and cut short at the ends or *couped* is the *baton* or *baston*, an ancient mark of illegitimacy which has become garbled as the 'bar sinister' – an obvious armorial impossibility. It has only rarely been used in Scotland.

The marginal illustrations show at a glance the ordinaries, some of their diminutives and the divisions of the field of the shield associated with them. So a shield divided in two horizontally is *parted per fess*; if vertically then *parted per pale*. With the exceptions of the pile and chief, a shield may be divided after any of the ordinaries. It may also be repeatedly subdivided as *barry*, *paly*, *bendy*, *bendy sinister*, *chevronny* and *pily*. It is acceptable and often very striking to combine two of these patterns; thus *barry-bendy* or *paly-bendy*. Paly-barry, as it would be, is called *chequy*, and bendy-bendy sinister becomes *lozengy*. A field divided per cross and per saltire, likewise becomes *gyronny* – the common feature in Campbell arms.

A field so repeatedly subdivided must specify the number of divisions, thus 'paly of eight'. The rule against colour on colour does not apply to divided fields as the sections are deemed to abut rather than to lie on one another (curiously the chief is also generally exempt as abutting rather than surmounting the rest of the shield). If an odd number is used, however, the rule applies as they then become diminutives of an ordinary placed upon a field. 'Paly of seven', cannot be; it is actually three pallets on a plain field and the rule applies. The rule is also partially suspended for ordinaries or charges laid over a divided field; for example, a chevron or a lion Gules could lie on a field barry Or and Azure but not on one barry Azure and Sable.

Subordinaries are essentially certain recognized standard geometric forms. They differ from ordinaries primarily in that multiples may be borne on a shield, they do not have diminutives and are not patterns for the division of a shield. The principal ones may be seen arranged in the marginal illustration.

The subordinary *bordure* or wide inner **border** of a shield carries especial notice for its importance in Scottish heraldry. In its simple form it is the principal engine of differencing arms within a family in Scotland. As will be seen in the next chapter, the use of bordures to indicate cadency is well established. The system of colours, the varying of the inner edge profile, dividing the border itself, and small charges placed upon it are all regular means of identifying branches of the same family.

A bordure does have diminutives. If very narrow and adjacent to the edge of the shield, it is a *fillet bordure*. If it is half its usual width and separated from the shield's perimeter so as to reveal the field between it and the edge, it is an *orle* and parallels the shape of the shield. If it is one half the width of an orle, it becomes a *tressure*.

One of the identifying aspects of Scots heraldry is the famous Royal Tressure. This is, as we shall see in Chapter 3, a double tressure showing fleurs-de-lys at regular intervals pointing alternately inwards and out, or *flory counter flory*. The number of flower heads has never been fixed but should never be fewer than six and preferably twice that or more.

Plate

Torteau

Bezant

Golpe

Orange

Hurt

Fountain

Pomme

Pellet

The Roundels

Bordure

Orle

Inescutcheon

Canton

Gyron

Flanches

Mascle

Billet

Fret

Lozenge

Fusil

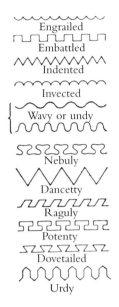

Engrailed
Embattled
Indented
Invected
Wavy or undy
Nebuly
Dancetty
Raguly
Potenty
Dovetailed
Urdy

Semé

In chief

Lord
Glendevon

Lines of Partition

Lines of partition and, indeed, the outlines of ordinaries and subordinaries can be drawn with varied, decorative lines. These standard outlines are often used both in composing new arms and in differencing existing arms as between family members or even between families. Thus the ancient arms of the House of Maxwell (Argent a saltire Sable) were distinguished from those of Colquhoun of Luss (Argent a saltire engrailed Sable) by the outline. They can lend a fine energy to the design and contribute much to the characteristic exuberance of heraldic art.

Charges

Charges are any other items to be placed upon the shield. They may be scattered uniformly over the shield, in which case it is said to be *semé* of the item. Thus, for example, a shield might be semé of roses. More often a certain number are stated, for example Argent three roses Gules, in which case they will automatically be placed two over one. If more are specified their arrangement should be blazoned: Argent nine roses Gules three three two and one. This is also necessary if they are to be specifically placed; thus Argent three roses Gules in chief, indicates they will be arranged in a straight line across the top part of the shield. Charges are presumed to lie upon the field. If they are to lie upon an ordinary it must so state in the blazon, and they will be evenly distributed on it. So, for example, the arms of the Rt Hon. John Adrian Hope, Baron Glendevon, were recorded in 1966 as Azure on a chevron Or between three bezants [gold discs], as many bay leaves paleways Vert.

Animals, real and mythical, of all species and kind, figure prominently in ancient and modern heraldry. A standard vocabulary of poses and postures has evolved for the beasts – and their bits – which will be part of the blazon's formula.

The ever popular **lion** is usually *rampant*, rearing up with three paws stretched out, but he and other beasts may also be *salient* (springing up but with both feet on the ground), *passant* (walking, usually with the right forepaw raised), *statant* (with all four feet down), *sejant* (sitting), and *couchant* (lying with head erect). Beasts are presumed to face the most honourable direction, thus to the dexter on a shield, to the hoist (pole) if on a flag, or to the altar if in a church. If they face out to the viewer, they are *gardant*, if looking back over the shoulder, *regardant*. If the whole beast faces forward it is *affronté*; thus the Royal Crest, a lion sejant affronté Gules.

The heads of beasts and birds are very popular charges. If cut close and smooth, a head is *couped*. If the neck is jagged it is *erased*. A head shown full faced and without any neck showing is termed *caboshed* – as the stag's head (*cabar feidh*) of the Mackenzies and the erstwhile Seaforth Highlanders. If the neck is shown, it will be *affronté* as is the stag's head crest of the Gordons and the former Gordon Highlanders.

Rampant

Salient gardant

Passant

Sejant

Couchant

Statant

LEFT:*Regimental badge of the former Seaforth Highlanders: a stag's head caboshed;*
RIGHT: *Regimental badge of the former Gordon Highlanders derived from the crest of the Marquess of Huntly, head of the House of Gordon: a stag's head affronté. The Seaforth, Gordon and Cameron Highlanders have now been amalgamated as 'The Highlanders' whose insignia incorporate the elements of its constituent regiments (United Scottish Services Museum).*

Birds are described as *close* (with the wings folded in), *rising* (with them raised) and *displayed* as is usual with eagles (fully frontal with both wings outstretched, tips up, talons stretched out on either side, tail spread and the head turned to the dexter). For artistic reasons the heads of birds are usually shown in profile, but the owl is always gardant (full face).

| Owl close | Eagle displayed | Hawk rising |

Care must be taken in choosing charges for a shield, bearing in mind the potential for the anachronistic or the simply ludicrous. Heraldry is, after all, symbolism, and an eagle will be much more satisfying to indicate an heroic fighter pilot's career, for example, than putting his aircraft on a medieval shield. Respect does not preclude humour, however, and armory is rich with delightful, often obscure, puns – called canting arms. Examples run from the ancient Argent cinquefoils or *fraises* (strawberry blossoms) of the Frasers, or Vert a lion rampant Argent, the poignant green field of Home, the great Border family, to those of Raeburn at page 14 and the very fresh turbot – Argent speckled fined and tailed Gules – of Mary Margaret Torbet recorded in 1964.

THE COMPONENTS OF AN ACHIEVEMENT

Once the arms have been established from the blazon, they can be reconstituted by an heraldic artist or craftsman in a myriad of wonderful ways and uses. The language of armory is especially esoteric and rich. Some blazons may be difficult – the more so because of confusing conventions of blazon in the past such as never repeating a tincture once stated. (The reader who wishes to study this aspect in detail will find suggestions for further reading listed at the back of the book.)

An **achievement** of arms is the term for the depiction of a shield painted with armorial bearings, surmounted by what is termed *timbre*: an appropriate helmet topped with the crest and draped with mantling, held in place at the base of the crest with a torse or an equivalent. If the owner of the arms is entitled to them, the achievement may also be flanked by supporters, depict insignia of office or honours, or sport a coronet of rank.

Achievement of Sir Alexander Stewart, Earl of Mar, 1408–1435, quartering his arms, first and fourth, with those of Mar, second and third. The shield is suspended, couché, by its leather guige or strap. The fine helmet with its simple mantling, crest-coronet and fearsome crest form an excellent armorial composition (Burnett).

The **shield** is the core of the achievement. Very possibly heraldic symbols first appeared on flags and pennons. The design is still called the *coat of arms* after the armorial patterned surcoat of the knight. Nonetheless, the shield is the enduring and proper figure for the display of the armorial bearings.

Great latitude may be allowed an heraldic artist in executing an achievement. The elements of a coat of arms are critical and cannot be varied, but the ways they are depicted or interpreted are freely open to the artist. Thus virtually any type or shape of shield – or shield analog such as a flag or sail or seat cushion – may be employed provided it adequately presents the arms. Historically, Scots women often displayed their arms on typical shields as well, but this practice fell into abeyance, and the custom of displaying them on a lozenge or diamond-shaped shield became usual. Latterly, the Lyon Court, while permitting the lozenge for females, has encouraged the use of the oval **cartouche**, considered both feminine and more practical for the depiction of armorial design.

The shield may be straight up or *couché*, tilted to the dexter in other words the viewer's left. The artist may chose to show the *guige* (shield strap) or not. The oval or lozenge is always shown upright and never with a strap. Very occasionally one will see two shields *accollée*, tilted in towards one another. This is done where one spouse's shield displays an honour such as the insignia of office or knighthood peculiar to that spouse, which is then inclined toward another shield carrying the impaled arms of both spouses together.

Sovereign's helm

Peer's helm

Knight's helm

Helm of a baron
or chief

Jousting helm

Pot helm

Sallet

*A display of the
conventional helms of
Scottish armory; drawn
for this work by the noted
Scots heraldic artist,
Romilly Squire.*

Helms, coronets and chapeaux

Helms and **coronets** proclaim the status of the *armiger* (the person whose arms are displayed) just as the arms themselves proclaim his or her identity. Usually shown resting atop the shield, both the helmet and the coronet, if a peer, follow established conventions of degree. The Sovereign uses a barred helmet of gold. A peer uses the same helmet, but of silver with gold bars. A knight or baronet may display a helmet with open visor or a jousting helm. In Scotland a feudal baron (as distinct from a peer in other words Lord of Parliament or baron), chiefs and heads of families may also use the tilting helm. Gentlemen display the steel pot helm or a closed visored steel helmet. Corporate bodies may use a sallet.

The **Sovereign's helm**, surmounted by the Crown and Royal Crest of, as appropriate, Scotland or England, is always displayed affronté. Other helms are usually shown facing to the dexter, but if the crest atop it is best shown full-on, the helm will be rotated front to accommodate it. Very occasionally two crests will be displayed, in which case two helms must be shown, as the Duke of Hamilton displays the crests of Douglas and of Hamilton as head of both those families.

Peers now commonly place their assigned **coronet of rank**, usually with its ermine-lined, gold-tasselled crimson cap of honour, directly on top of the shield with their silver helm resting in turn on top of the coronet and cap. This is colourful but rather unconvincing as the coronet must be drawn wash-tub sized to accommodate the helm squashing down on it, a necessary exception to the commendable modern practice of drawing the helm, shield and crest in roughly true, that is equal, proportions. The silly and quite impossible 'duck bill' helmets of the 18th and 19th centuries are happily history.

As drawn, a duke's coronet shows five stylised strawberry leaves, that of a marquess three and two silver ball 'pearls' (no actual gems of any sort are allowed on peers' coronets). The earl sports no less than five balls on stalks between four leaves. A viscount's coronet is a chased band with nine balls visible and resting on the rim, while a baron's is a plain circlet showing four balls.

These coronets were fixed by the Stuart kings in the 17th century. At his coronation, **Charles I** also authorised the feudal barons of Scotland to attend wearing no coronet but a cap of degree edged with ermine. Today, feudal barons and 'chiefs of the name and arms' are entitled to display this tassel-topped cap immediately above the shield as peers do their coronets. A further singular feature of Scots heraldry is that these baronial caps are depicted Gules if the family retains the feudal superiority or possession, but Azure if they are the representer of the family which previously was associated with the barony. Also unique is the practice of painting this cap as lined contre ermine, that is black with white tail spots, where the barony was originally held under authority other than the Crown.

Quite similar in appearance but of an altogether different nature are the *crest-coronets*. These are not coronets of rank but of art, used instead of a torse or heraldic chapeau as a base for the crest where it joins the mantling and helmet. The most common is the misnamed 'ducal coronet', which certainly has nothing to do with being a duke. It is a generic sort of medieval element usually featuring three strawberry leaves on a decorated band and rim. They are often blazoned in colour to minimise confusion with the golden coronets of rank and are rarely granted these days. Other crest-coronets included the plain spiked ancient or antique crown, the mural crown, naval, astral and celestial crown – all non-nobiliary coronets though usually granted allusively in recognition of some highly distinguished service.

In addition to coronets of rank and crest-coronets, Scotland enjoys a lively tradition of **civic coronets**. These are changing to reflect the reorganisations in local government. Early in the 20th century, burghs ensigned their arms with the picturesque and apt burghal coronet, similar to the mural one of masonry, coloured to reflect their status. A county council was entitled to a green coronet of five points interspersed with four gold *garbs* or sheaves. In 1975 a series was devised for the new authorities with regional councils receiving a band chased with saltires and surmounted with thistles; district

Ducal	Ancient	Celestial
Astral	Naval	Vallary

Pre 1975

Royal Burgh

Police Burgh

Burgh of Barony

County Council
Post 1975

Regional Council

District Council
Post 1996

City Council

Council

Island Council

Community
Council

Full achievement of the Perth and Kinross Council showing its unique double eagle supporter and the new Council Coronet. From the Public Register of All Arms and Bearings by courtesy of the Lyon Office: painted by Mrs Patricia Bertram (Hodgson).

councils displayed five thistle heads without the leaves, while the Island councils sported two dolphins and the community councils showed two pine cones between three thistle leaves (possibly those stripped from the district councils). In 1996 regional councils and their coronets were done away with. The new coronets are all gold without a chased band. The Islands and community councils' format remains otherwise the same. The cities of Aberdeen, Dundee, Edinburgh and Glasgow will be entitled to golden burghal coronets. The remaining councils will revert to the handsome former county coronet of five points interspersed with four garbs, now all gold, the garbs bound sable.

LEFT: *Silver crest of Mac Dhòmnuill, the Lord Macdonald, Chief of Clan Donald, to be worn in his bonnet and showing the three eagle's feathers of a chief and his baron's coronet on a plain circlet;*
RIGHT: *the heraldic coronet, helm, crest and motto of Lord Macdonald;*
BELOW: *his crest enclosed within a strap and buckle and used as a badge by his clansmen to denote allegiance to him (Dennis).*

Crests

Crests cause a great deal of confusion in Scotland as elsewhere. Too often the term is used comprehensively and wrongly for the arms or even the whole achievement. It properly relates only to the device designed to crest the helmet – historically probably only actually worn at tournaments and for display.

The crest, once in fact and now in theory, is modelled in the round and joined to the helmet at the *torse* or wreath, a stylised twisted skein of cloth which binds the mantling in place on the helmet. Alternatively the crest may rise out of a crest coronet or rest upon a stylised heraldic hat called a *chapeau*, like the baronial cap but without a tassel. It is not accepted heraldic practice to use a torse in conjunction with either of these.

A common usage is to display the crest on its torse (or chapeau or crest-coronet), floating alone without the helm or shield. This is not objectionable. However, Scots enjoy an interesting rule for crests which reflects their strong sense of family and clan. Whereas in England each person is theoretically obliged to difference not only his arms

LEFT: *Mr T C Manson, Officer to the Faculty of Advocates, Edinburgh, wearing his dress coat with crested buttons and the silver badge of the arms of the Faculty;* RIGHT: *the badge illustrates the ancient practice of retainers in displaying allegiance and is believed to be the source of the symbolic strap and buckle now so usual in clansmen's badges (Hodgson).*

but his crest as well, in Scotland the arms are carefully differenced, but the crests may be shared, undifferenced, throughout the family. Thus the shield will be much more personal than one's crest for stationery and other similar uses.

Additionally, the crest may double as a man's badge. A **badge** is intended as a device which may be worn by one's household or followers to indicate affiliation. By long tradition in Scotland, a follower may display his allegiance by wearing the crest of his superior as a badge within a circular strap and buckle device. This is the familiar clansman's cap badge featuring the crest of his chief within the strap and buckle, usually bearing the chief's slogan or motto. It must be stressed this is a badge of affiliation only and no armorial right is thereby conferred. It is not the 'clan crest' or 'my crest as a MacQuatnaught'; it is the personal crest of the chief, worn publicly as a badge to proclaim ones allegiance to him. When the clans were a force with which to be reckoned rather than a collective notion, the identifying badges actually employed seem to have been plants, a sprig of which might be fixed in the bonnet as a badge. These plant badges still figure frequently in Highland achievements and are festive features worn at gatherings today.

A *duine uasail* – 'a gentleman of coat armour' or armiger – will wear his own crest, alone or on a plain circlet with his motto. Alternatively, he might chose to wear his chief's crest within a strap and buckle. He may also display the clan plant badge and a single golden eagle feather, making all in all for a bulky bonnet. An armiger's crest (or arms) may also handsomely be displayed in Highland dress on his sporran, buttons, buckles, brooch and arms.

Beyond this use of the crest as a badge, **personal badges**, as distinct emblems, are not often granted or used in Scotland though the Officers of Arms now have individual badges as do some heads of great houses and clan chiefs. Corporate bodies, on the other hand, be they local government, schools, companies or sports clubs, are making increasing use of the heraldic badge as a most appropriate means for a member to display affiliation.

Mottoes

Mottoes probably arose from the *cri de guerre* or some memorable utterance or incident, then in calmer times took on the nature of an edifying sentiment. They are part of heritable armorial rights in Scotland and, while not necessarily fixed, tend not to be altered over time, even when they cease to be particularly intelligible!

By custom the cadet or junior branches choose mottoes or slogans which relate to that of the head of the family or 'answer it'. Thus the Scott Dukes of Buccleuch proclaim broadly '*Amo*' (I love – an undoubted battle cry), while Scott of Thirlstane advertises 'Ready, aye ready!' and Scott of Harden grounds things again with '*Pacem amo*' (I love peace).

Many families share the same mottoes, often of an elevating note. So, among others, Learmonth, MacLennan, Logan and the Royal Burgh of St Andrews all hope while they breathe – '*Dum spiro spero*'. In Latin or Gaelic the families of MacDougal, MacDowall, Maclaine, and MacNeil each hazard all with 'Victory or death!' Mottoes can also prove an irresistible opportunity for the recondite punster: thus Hope intones '*At spes non fracta*' (Yet Hope is not broken) and '*Festina lente*' (Make haste slowly) cheers on Lord Onslow.

War cries, rallying points, and famous epigrams all figure in Scottish mottoes. These are customarily drawn in a suitable **scroll** over the crest. English achievements place the motto below the shield, but this is done in Scotland only when there are two or more mottoes or slogans displayed in the achievement, one above and one below, or where there is no crest, as is common with corporate arms.

Mantling

Mantling is the drapery fixed to the helmet, by tradition to shield it from the sun's rays in the Crusades. Also called the *capeline* or *lambrequin*, the first examples of it are quite simple, often being an attractive continuation of the crest, as the fur coat of an animal head crest, or sometimes bearing the arms themselves.

From the late 16th century the **drapery** becomes the artist's delight, whipped and curled and flounced to fill any gap in the achievement. So overwrought and exuberant did this become that the artists seem to have become confused as to its very nature, and examples exist of it depicted as plumage or baroque acanthus foliage. At this time, too, the habit of depicting all mantling as red lined with white, *Gules doubled Argent*, replaced the earlier custom of the mantling being of the principal colour lined with the principal metal. The wreath or torse, however, generally continued to be shown in the main colour/metal combination, the livery colours of the family.

In 1891 the old practice was reinstituted. From that date on, the mantling has been officially blazoned and depicted as of the livery colours. The torse is conventionally shown with six twists, alternating the primary metal with primary colour. Peers, however, continue to mantle their helms with crimson lined with ermine, presumably an allusion to their coronation robes, though the torses will be of their liveries. The Sovereign displays cloth of gold doubled ermine, and no torse is shown as the helm is surmounted with the Crown.

There is some movement toward allowing more artistic variation in the mantling now it has been reduced to an intelligible state. Thus it might now be blazoned as semé, strewn, of small figures, or veined. This was certainly done in the 14th century, and can be very effective if restrained. Likewise the torse, chapeau or crest-coronets were once just alternatives to other livelier solutions to the join of crest to mantling, including wreaths of flowers, of leaves, ribbons or banderolles, a gold chain or, indeed, where appropriate, nothing at all – as where the gown of a human crest figure might continue on as the mantling.

Scottish arms from the Armorial del Gelre of about 1380 showing the variety of medieval mantling. FROM THE TOP: Lord of Annandale, Sir James Sandelands of Calder and Sir Patrick Hepburn.

Supporters

Supporters are the men, beasts or, rarely, objects which flank the shield and ostensibly 'support' it. Their use arose much later than coat armour and the crest as part of a general transfer of the art of heraldry from the round to the flat, from the actual object, be it a shield, helmet and crest, draped mantling, or banner, to a picture of the object as part of a decorative display. A useful artistic addition to fill in the spaces at the sides, especially on seals, they lend an extra grandeur to a pictorial display.

Supporters can be seen in the famous pairing of the lion and the unicorn in the royal arms. Their presence is generally expected by the wider public, yet one of the first clues that an achievement may be bogus is their, usually regal, appearance as, in fact, the right to supporters is rare and jealously guarded. As a general rule only peers of the realm, Knights of the Thistle and Garter or Knights and Dames

A recent achievement granted to the University of Strathclyde, Glasgow, and formally presented on 13 January 1996. Note the unusual shape of shield (Strathclyde University).

Grand Cross of the other orders of chivalry (for their lifetime only), certain departments of government, and corporate bodies granted royal charters or created by Act of Parliament are entitled to them. In Scotland, however, some families have made out an ancient prescriptive right to them, as well as certain chiefs and feudal barons, and even a few high officials. In all, a small fraction of those with a right to bear and display arms are allowed supporters. The right to supporters is personal, and does not descend to cadet houses, though in Scotland the immediate heir apparent may, of courtesy, also display them.

Supporters are required to stand on either the precarious edge of a lower motto scroll or, a better practice, on a patch of ground below the shield termed the compartment. This is presumed to be a plain grassy knoll, but there are rare instances where the head of a family has a special compartment specified in the Patent of Arms. Thus the Earl of Perth, head of the Drummonds, strews his compartment with the devilish caltrop – spiked devices to lame the enemy's destriers, Dundas of that Ilk toasts his shield over a flaming salamander, and Struan Robertson, Chief of Clan Donnachaidh, places his over a prostrate wild man in chains. Even if not so blazoned, the compartment will often be depicted growing a crop of the appropriate plant badge of the family or clan. The royal arms, for example, usually feature the national plant badges of thistles, roses, shamrocks and sometimes daffodils or leeks.

Insignia

Insignia of office and of honour may also figure in an achievement. Scotland is especially rich in the official insignia of her hereditary and professional **office bearers**; the Duke of Argyll crosses in saltire behind his shield the ceremonial baton as Hereditary Master of the Queen's Household, a red rod semé of golden thistles and topped with the Crown and Royal Crest, with the naked sword of the Hereditary Chief Justiciar of Argyll (an office, if not a dignity, actually long abolished). Crossing such symbols of office in saltire behind the shield is a much favoured design. The Governor of Edinburgh Castle crosses a key ensigned with a castle and Royal Crown, with a sword as General Officer

The Duke of Argyll
Master of the Royal Household

Earl of Mar and Kellie
Keeper of Stirling Castle

Commanding for Scotland (see p.49). The hereditary keepers of Stirling Castle and Falkland Palace likewise cross keys with batons of their office. Pursuivants and heralds of arms cross their ebony batons behind their shields, and so also the Lord Lyon displays his beautiful gold and blue enamel baton of office embellished with thistles, roses, harps, and the last vestigial fleurs-de-lys,

Sir Crispin Agnew of Lochnaw, BT, QC Rothesay Herald

symbols of the ancient claim to the throne of France, in official use.

The faithful Gilbert le Hay was tipped by King Robert the Bruce to be High Constable of Scotland in 1315 and today his heir Merlin, Earl of Erroll, as Lord High Constable crosses silver batons tipped with gold in saltire behind his shield and also displays the odd

Earl of Erroll
Lord High Constable

and ancient emblem of the Constable, two armoured hands issuing from clouds at each side of the base of the shield holding bared swords erect and flanking it.

The Earl of Dundee as Chief of the Scrymgeours, is hereditary Royal Banner Bearer – as his forbearers have been for nearly nine centuries, even before the Lion was adopted –

Earl of Dundee
Royal Banner Bearer

and displays the lion rampant banners of the sovereign crossed in saltire behind his shield. The Earls of Lauderdale for some time disputed this right, but in a laudable compromise are now recognised as hereditary bearer for the sovereign of the national banner of Scotland and cross two national flags, Azure a saltire Argent, the cross of St Andrew, behind their shield.

Earl of Lauderdale
National Banner Bearer

The **churches** of Scotland also use armorial insignia to distinguish their offices. The Moderator of the General Assembly of the Church of Scotland has two official achievements, the greater displays his arms of office featuring the

Moderator of the
Church of Scotland

burning bush of the Church (impaled with the Moderator's personal arms if he is, as he indeed should be, armigerous), with a representation of the ancient *cuigrich*, the crozier of St Fillan, in pale behind the shield which is ensigned by the delightful adaptation of a black Geneva bonnet or 'John Knox cap' with the addition of twenty tassels arranged ten to a side, like an archbishop. The lesser achievement simply places the shield within a purple jewelled ring, symbolic of the Moderator's ring. Any clergyman may display a plain black priest's hat with one black tassel a side in lieu of a helmet and crest. Episcopal bishops will place their jewelled mitre above the shield, and Roman Catholic bishops may display the mitre

Episcopal Bishop

together with a crozier and processional cross in saltire behind the shield. They may also place their many tasselled episcopal hats over the whole achievement.

Baronets will place the arms of Nova Scotia or the 'bloody hand of Ulster', as appropriate to their creation, either on a canton or escutcheon on the shield, or the badge suspended from a ribbon below the shield. Similarly, **knights** may display their appropriate badge below the shield, and Knights and Dames Grand Cross of an order and Knights of the Thistle and of the Garter may surround their shield with the collar of their order. Certain classes

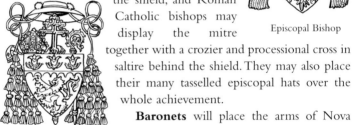

Roman Catholic
Cardinal Archbishop

Earl of Dalhousie
Knight of the Thistle

of the Order of St John and the Knights of Malta may also display their respective insignia (see p.95). Holders of significant honours and decorations may depict them suspended from their proper ribbon below the shield. As a general rule, if the decoration entitles the holder to the use of its initials after his or her

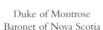

Duke of Montrose
Baronet of Nova Scotia

name, it may appear on the achievement. All these emphasize the role of arms as personal identification as well as visually celebrating the contributions of that individual to the life of the nation.

THE ARMS OF HER MAJESTY'S LORD LYON KING OF ARMS

Achievement of the arms of office of the Lord Lyon King of Arms. The enamelled baton of office appears twice in token of his office as King of Arms and again as the King of Arms of the Order of the Thistle. The arms are flanked by his lion supporters, encircled with a collar of thistle and rue, a triple chain of gold, and ensigned with the Lyon's crown of office. This version was painted by the late Don Pottinger.

The armes of ye twa queynis sporusit to king James ye fift
ye first was magdalene de france; ye secund marie de lorane.

Magdalene qtheyne.   Marie: queyne,

CHAPTER 2

THE DESCENT OF ARMS

'A'rms', wrote the learned Alexander Nisbet, 'are a silent name'. Having been introduced to the basic rules of armory, let us look at how they are applied in crafting arms for the person.

The simplest form of the arms of a family may descend without differencing from father to eldest son forever. All other members of the family will alter their arms to distinguish them. *Marshalling* is the art of ordering an individual's arms to reflect his antecedents and status.

If it would be ludicrous to propose that all Stuarts be named James; just so with arms. The basic elements of the arms – the Stuart part – remain essentially constant, but are differenced to reflect the individual identity and lineage of the owner, for example the John, James or Angus part of a name. As with names, too, the family and descent may be restated in the arms, the present expression of the past and promise of the future.

In Scotland we begin with the proposition that all of the same **surname** may be assumed to be at least 'Scotch cousins', that is, related at some point now beyond our record or recollection. This sense of the bond of family is essential to armory and almost certainly explains not only its survival but its expansion in this increasingly anonymous and fragmented age. If, therefore, one is a Campbell, one's arms will almost certainly be based on the instantly recognisable gyronny pattern common to them; if a Cameron, expect some variation of Gules three bars Or, and so on.

OPPOSITE: Folio from the armorial manuscript of Sir David Lindsay of the Mount, with the arms of the two queens of James V, Madeleine de Valois, Princess of France, d. 1537, and Marie de Lorraine whom he married in 1538. They are depicted on lozenges, impaling the royal arms of the King of Scots with the arms of their fathers, respectively King of France and Duke of Guise.

Duke of Argyll, Mac Cailean Mór, chief of the name and arms of Campbell: the plain arms of Campbell ensigned with a Duke's coronet.

Arms of Captain J H D M Campbell as recorded in 1929, differenced with a border chequy.

Arms of the Revd Wm James Cameron, recorded in 1964 and differenced with a bend and charges.

Cameron of Locheil, Mac Dhomnuill Duibh, chief of the name and arms of Cameron: the arms of Cameron ensigned with the Cap of Estate of a chief or feudal baron.

WOOD NOTES WILD

BETTER A WEE BUSH THAN NÆ BIELD

Robert Burns fancied himself 'a bit of a herald' and designed these arms for his own use. Though he never recorded them they were subsequently incorporated into proper grants to relatives. The shepherd's hornpipe and crook emphasis the pastoral theme, and the bush reflects the unusual second motto.

Chart of brisures or temporary house marks of cadency used by children by courtesy, that is, without formal authority of the Lyon Office, until they establish houses and families of they own. They will then matriculate their arms with proper and permanent differences as assigned by the Lord Lyon. From Alexander Nisbet's System of Heraldry, *1722.*

It is for the Lord Lyon to determine how the arms are to be composed, if newly granted, and differenced if derived from an existing coat. The first is by means of a formal **Petition** for Grant of Ensigns Armorial. The second is by petition for Cadet-Matriculation of Arms. In less settled times this was sometimes avoided, and the bizarre results led to repeated acts of parliament to control armorial practice through the court of the Lord Lyon.

Technically, a grant of arms from the Lord Lyon is a patent of what may be thought of as minor nobility; the grantee is thereby 'enrolled with all nobles in the noblesse of Scotland'. This is perhaps more akin to the word 'gentility' in its modern sense – notable rather than strictly noble. It certainly does not constitute a peerage patent, nor is it necessarily evidence of anything other than that the grantee is, in the language of the statute, a 'vertuous and well-deserving Persone', no small thing. 'The rank is but the guinea's stamp', Burns reminds us: 'The man's the gowd for a' that'.

ARMS AND THE MAN

The eldest son will succeed to the undifferenced arms of his father. In Scotland arms are heritage, are property, and being indivisible are implicitly limited to inheritance by the senior heir of the name unless, of course, otherwise entailed or tailzied, that is with an explicit destination to, say, heir-male of the body or next collateral heir-male. During the lifetime of the head of the family, his senior son (or other heir-presumptive) will display the arms with a traverse bar with three downward tabs, a label; his grandson will display one with five tabs, and so on. On his death, his son succeeds to the arms

The Minute differences.

1ˢᵗ the Labell.	2. the Crescent.	3. the Mollet.	4. the Martlet.
6. the Flower de lis	7. the Rose.	8. the Cross Moline.	9. the Anchor.

and discards the label, and each eldest son of the next generations will move up one label.

Younger sons may display their father's arms with a *brisure*, a house-mark or temporary mark of cadency, of courtesy, until they reach full age, marry or set up an independent household. They then will matriculate as a **cadet** house. No cadet may simply adopt what he thinks fitting – there is no Do-It-Yourself armory in Scotland as in England and elsewhere. The Act of 1592, still law, obliges the 'lyoun king-of-armes, and his brether herauldis...to distinguische and discerne thame with congruent differences, and thairefter to matriculat tham in thair buikis and Registeris'. They are still faithfully doing so.

There are a number of means of differencing arms for cadets, but the usual system, most fully developed and long successfully employed in Scotland, is the use of **bordures** (armorial borders), permanent and inheritable marks of cadency. The basic formula is set out in the illustration. There is a general system of priority of tinctures and lines. Thus bordures might be assigned as first Or then Argent, Gules and on to Azure. The inner edge of a bordure or the edges of the principal ordinary may be varied as engrailed, then invected, then indented. Allowance must be made, however, for the design of each shield, and these are only starting points. Where, for example, the usual difference would be a border of the same tincture as the field, it may be assigned as chequy of the principal metal and colour. Thus the Rt Hon Sir Malcolm Innes of Edingight, Lord Lyon King of Arms, bears for Innes Argent three mullets (stars) Azure, but, as a third son's bordure Argent would have been invisible on a field Argent, it is a lively chequy Argent and Azure.

The system of coloured borders (bordures) at work. The father as head of the family bears the arms undifferenced, perhaps Argent a fess Vert. The eldest son flaunts a removable label. The younger sons will be assigned permanent borders according to their birth order. His wife may display her husband's arms by courtesy (Dennis).

More remote relationship will generally be indicated by the Lord Lyon by altering the elements of the basic arms. The number, colour or kind of charges may be varied, or an ordinary may be added, moved or altered. Occasionally the overall colour scheme may be changed or reversed. Throughout, however, a reference to the arms of the head of the family will be preserved.

ARMS AND THE LADY

It is very much a time of development in arms for women as they succeed to traditionally male positions and the use of arms within them. While historically arms, and the law of arms, have been largely a male province, women have always transmitted and carried the arms of father or husband. Indeed, the medieval custom of wearing them on kirtle and mantle is easily as splendidly dramatic as waving them in a battle.

Men in their official capacity have usually displayed only their paternal arms, but a woman cannot well use her husband's arms – which she certainly may do socially – in an official capacity on a shield of office, say as Governor of Edinburgh Castle or as Moderator of the Church of Scotland. There would be no way of distinguishing his arms from hers. Should she use her maiden arms the confusion shifts to whether it is her father or herself that is represented. No doubt the heraldic authority will resolve this as it has all other social developments of the last eight centuries; in the interim, women make do with their characteristic oval.

A female is entitled, by right of courtesy, to bear her father's undifferenced arms prior to her marriage, during it in conjunction with her husband's (or without his as she chooses), and as a widow

Three royal couples from the Forman of Luthrie Armorial. BELOW: *James I and his queen, Joan Beaufort;*
OPPOSITE TOP: *James III and his queen, Margaret of Denmark;*
OPPOSITE BOTTOM: *Mary Queen of Scots and her husband, Francis II, King of France (Lyon Office).*

to bear her maiden or her former husband's arms. As in other areas, Scots women have historically enjoyed a good deal of autonomy in these matters, even displaying their arms on shields rather than the traditional **lozenge**. It is quite similar to the way women have maintained their surnames in Scots law. In recent times, an effort has been made to encourage the adoption of the oval **cartouche** for the arms of Scots women, as being handsome and practical, rather than the awkward and angular lozenge.

If an armiger has no sons, his eldest

daughter as heir of the line may succeed to the indivisible right of his undifferenced arms provided she keeps his surname and that the arms are not otherwise tailzied. She will then bear them in her person and transmit them to her child together with that surname, thus preserving the name and arms of the senior branch of the family. This is not a matter of usage by courtesy but a right in the law of succession as the daughter is now the senior representative of the line. Likewise her sisters may petition the Lord Lyon for properly differenced versions of their father's arms exactly as their brothers might. These younger sisters may then pass their duly differenced cadet arms to their children as well.

It has thus been quite common in the ancient families when the only heir is a daughter for her husband and their children to voluntarily assume her name and arms. It is also not unusual for such inheritances to include a compulsory 'name and arms' clause, an *entail*, requiring the beneficiary to adopt the names and arms of the benefactor. He must then surrender up his patrilineal name and arms and assume the new ones by Lyon Court interlocutor. Alternatively if permitted by the terms of the entail, he might hyphenate both surnames and apply to quarter the arms with his own.

In Scotland a female is as equally entitled to a new grant of arms as any male and may, subject to the terms of the Patent of Arms, pass them to her children. The Lyon Office frowns on a grant of a crest to a woman unless there are extenuating circumstance, but male heirs of the grantee will usually be designated as entitled to the use of a crest. A peeress in her own right or chief of a clan will enjoy the same rights to crest, slogan and supporters as a male. She will, however, not display a helmet on the achievement on the premise she would not wear one to war.

MARSHALLING – MARRIAGE, DESCENT AND OFFICE

Marriage and descent

Marriage and descent pose related problems. During marriage a wife may display her husband's arms on an oval or lozenge. As his widow she may continue to do so but will surround the arms with a *cordeliere*, a black cord. If her father was armigerous, she may chose to use either husband's or father's arms, or, most usually, will *impale* them – that is, the shield will be split vertically in half, along the palar line. The husband's arms will conventionally be placed in the dexter and the wife's maiden arms in the sinister side. The whole of both arms will be shown, though any bordure or tressure will stop at the palar line.

Children will ordinarily bear the arms of their father alone, differenced between them as has been mentioned. If their mother has no brother, or one who leaves no children, she may become an heraldic heiress and transmit her father's arms to her issue. If she is the eldest sister or only child, as representative of the family her child will necessarily succeed to the maternal surname as well as the undifferenced arms of the maternal grandfather. Alternatively, if the mother has matriculated arms as a younger sister (as discussed above) or has been granted arms herself, she may pass them on to her children as well. In these cases this will ordinarily be done by the Lord Lyon quartering the shield of the eldest male and placing the father's arms in the first and fourth quarters and the mother's (or mother's father's duly differenced) in the second and third. Current practice is for the younger children of such a union to difference the arms of their father in the conventional manner then place them in the first and fourth quarters with their mother's, without further difference, in the second and third. Arms when quartered display the entire bordure within its quarter, so these will clearly be seen as, say, the third son of a man married to an heraldic heiress. The Lord Lyon

may assign this child's children, in turn, their respective bordures around the entire quartered shield – thus proclaiming, for example, the armiger as the second son of the third son of a man who married an heraldic heiress.

There are slow vogues in heraldry as in other esoterica. In the last two centuries it seemed engrandising and good to display as many arms of relationship as possible. Examples exist of dozens even scores of arms crammed into a vast shield. Scotland never succumbed to the worst of this often excessive practice of pretence, conspired in by some of the more accommodating English heralds. Scottish practice permits each quarter to be quartered and no more. This is called grand-quarters. Theoretically this would allow the classic summum bonum of *seize quartiers*, the 16 quarters indicating that the person's parents, grandparents, great-grandparents and great-great-grandparents were all armigerous, were all 'noble'. In fact, the chances of all the women being heraldic heiresses is nominal! The pendulum has swung, however, and there is a very proper resistance in the Lyon Court to unnecessary multiplicity of quarterings. Thus many of the oldest families prefer to use the simplest and oldest patrilineal coat alone.

A note may be entered here regarding the armorial practices of the Western Isles and Highlands where the use of standard heraldry came late. Many of the magnates of those areas, not to be outshone by their much quartered countrymen in the south, assumed quartered coats at the onset. (Interestingly, most people asked to design a 'coat of arms' for themselves will start by quartering the shield.) These Highland quarterings may be thought of as totemic rather than dynastic. The galley of the Isles, the lion, the eagle, couped hands, salmon and castles appear in most of these in one form or another. Doubtless these families were interrelated, but the symbols are more shared than inherited. Such a quartered coat is regarded as *unum quid* (indivisible) and treated as a simple coat would be in marshalling arms.

Inescutcheons

The arms of the Lyon Office impaling those of Sir Thomas Innes of Learney, displayed in a very effective late medieval manner on a banner held by a single supporter and here ensigned with the crown of office of the Lord Lyon King of Arms. The work of the late Don Pottinger (Hodgson).

Inescutcheons are small shields superimposed centrally over the arms on a larger shield. In Scotland they are used in a number of instances. Where, for example, there is a much quartered and grand-quartered shield, the principal arms of the family might be featured alone on the 'inescutcheon overall'. If the armiger holds a particular fief or territory or the chiefship of a clan, those arms may be placed on an inescutcheon. Over the centuries some families have been granted Augmentations of Honour in the forms of inescutcheons, as well. These inescutcheons are frequently *ensigned*, that is topped, by a coronet of rank or even, as a mark of royal favour, the Crown itself. An example of this may be seen in the arms of the Earl of Mar and Kellie on p.36.

Lastly, inescutcheons are used as an alternative to the canton for displaying the arms of Nova Scotia or the red hand of Ulster of a baronet. The arms of Agnew of Lochnaw, on p.37, display a baronet's inescutcheon. The English practice of placing the arms of an heraldic heiress on an 'escutcheon of pretence' over her husband's arms does not obtain in Scotland.

Impalements of office

Impalements of office are similar to the domestic impalement noted above. The shield will be divided vertically, but the office's arms will be placed in the dexter half with those of the office holder in the sinister. These are temporary in the sense that they are current and proper only whilst the office is held. If, for shame, the office holder is not armigerous and refuses to obtain arms, the arms of office may be borne by him or her alone and without impalement.

Examples of **official arms** which may be impaled would be those of the Office of the Lord Lyon, the Moderator of the Church of Scotland, any of the bishoprics and abbacies of the Episcopal or Roman Catholic Churches, General Officer Commanding and Governor of Edinburgh Castle, or the Principal of Strathclyde University. A number of kirk sessions within the Church of Scotland have received grants of arms. The minister is permitted their use while serving that church and may display them complete with the traditional black hat and tassels.

Additionally, it would be appropriate to request permission of the Lord Lyon to impale the arms of a company with those of its president, a city and its lord provost, a trades incorporation and its deacon, a professional organisation and its chairman, a university and its chancellor and so on, basically in any circumstance where there is an armigerous corporate body and an armigerous executive head of it.

Though not strictly an impalement, knights and dames at the higher levels of the Order of St John and the Knights of Malta are permitted to add a chief of the arms of the respective orders to their personal arms.

These are all splendid practices as they rehearse the dignity of the office at the same time as celebrating the accomplishments of the person holding it. Thus the institution and the individuals most to be identified with it are published and handsomely commemorated.

The official arms of Lt Gen Sir Derek Lang KCB as the Governor of Edinburgh Castle: official arms on dexter, personal arms on sinister (Burnett).

49

CHAPTER 3

THE LION AND THE CROWN

I n Scotland all heraldic authority derives from the Crown. It is exercised by the Sovereign's depute, the Lord Lyon King of Arms, whose title comes from the ancient unchanging symbol of Scotland's sovereignty, the rampant red lion 'on his field of tressured gold'.

OPPOSITE: *A charming if naive achievement of the royal arms of James VI and I, carved and painted in wood for use in Scotland, c. 1605. Despite its irregular quarterings, it nonetheless makes its royal point (Historic Scotland).*

THE ROYAL ARMS OF SCOTLAND

We cannot date with certainty when the **lion** was allied with the Crown. In the first decades of armory there was no central control. It seems clear that armorial devices were initially asssumed and abandoned at will by the persons concerned. The King of Scots at this time was William the Lion, who reigned from 1165 to 1214. Circumstantially it appears it was William who adopted the red rampant lion as the arms of Scotland's king. It does not appear on his seal, but that would have been cut at the start of his reign before the sudden rise in armory in the last quarter of the 12th century. It certainly appears on the seal of his son and successor, Alexander II, and has been borne by all subsequent kings and queens of Scots.

The King of England at this time, Richard the Lionheart, a friend of William the Lion, also adopted arms at this period. Initially he bore a shield with two lions *rampant combatant* (rearing up and facing one another) before opting, in about 1195, for the three lions *passant guardant*, heraldic leopards, that is, in a walking position and facing out at the viewer, still borne for England.

Seal of Alexander II: in fine medieval style the King is depicted armed and mounted; the rampant lion can be made out on his shield and horse trappings.

Scottish lions from the Scots Roll drawn some time between 1455 and 1490. The arms, described in the original spellings, are, from the top: The Kyng of Scottes, Crochton of Sanchar, Sr Dauid Dunbar, Erle of ffyfe, Mowbray.

The lion obviously had great appeal as a symbol of personal ferocity and dignity and, in its role as King of Beasts, temporal sovereignty. It was widely adopted throughout Europe and within Scotland. In addition to the ancient territories of Fife (a red lion on a gold shield) and Galloway (a crowned white lion on blue), the lion rampant forms the dynastic arms of Dunbar (white on red), Home (white on green), Lamont (white on blue), Macdowall (crowned white on blue), Moubray (crowned white on red), Dundas (red on white), Crichton (blue on white), more recently still the Scottish Motor Trade Association Ltd (black upon white) and, with various additions, of many, many more.

The lion of the ancient Celtic earldom or kingdom of **Fife** (red on gold) is of especial interest. This is now borne by the Wemyss family as successors to the Macduffs, ancient Celtic kings of Fife and also by the current Duke of Fife (Chief of the Carnegies) in right of his fief of Fife. The royal arms, of course, feature a similar red lion rampant on a field of gold but within a red *double tressure flory counter flory* – that is two very narrow parallel borders with fleurs de lys alternately pointing inwards and out. Ordinarily this, as an additional figure on a shield, would indicate a junior line or cadet house. The general rule is: the simpler the arms, the older and more senior the house. This does not appear to have been a conscious allusion in this case, however. One school of thought suggests it is simply derived from an ornamental but structural strengthening rim of a shield.

A far more poetic tradition maintains it was granted by the Emperor Charlemagne, *c.* 800, to King Achaius of the Scots in gratitude for his alliance and in token that, as the Scottish lion had come to the aid of France, the lilies of France would henceforth protect and defend Scotland; another theory holds that it derived from the ribbons of Charlemagne's daughters, binding lilies about their brows. Sadly there can be no literal truth in these tales, but their poetical and political impulse may be admired.

The double tressure flory counter flory, whatever its provenance, has come to be strongly associated with Scottish heraldry, and, more particularly, with its royal house. It would not now be granted except by royal warrant, and where it is found, in any of its colour variations, it may be inferred that at some point there has been a marriage with the royal house or some very remarkable service to warrant its grant from the Crown.

The precise nature of the royal arms may be difficult to understand. They are at once personal, the arms of the Sovereign, and territorial, the arms of sovereignty. It is wrong to speak of the 'arms of Scotland' or the 'arms of the United Kingdom'. They are the arms of the royal house, of the King of Scots, and now of the Queen of the United Kingdom of Great Britain and Northern Ireland. It is thus incorrect to use the lion rampant as the flag of Scotland; it is a royal banner of her sovereign who has, however, issued a Royal Warrant permitting its display as a token of loyalty to the Crown. The national flag is the saltire of St Andrew. It is also wrong to call it the Stuart lion: it was the ensign of the King of Scots long before the Stuarts were Scotland's kings, and if one ceases to be king, he also loses the right to the royal arms.

Thus when in 1292 John **Balliol** was adjudged closest in right to the throne vacated by the untimely death of the child Queen Margaret, the Maid of Norway, he put aside his own arms and bore the tressured lion as king. When he subsequently defied Edward I's presumptions, the English king literally had the lion cut from Balliol's coat thus earning him the sobriquet 'Toom Tabard (literally, empty coat of arms)'.

In 1306 Robert the **Bruce** assumed the lion with the crown. The arms he had hitherto borne as Lord of Annandale (Or a saltire and a chief Gules), still survive in the arms of the Bruce Earls of Elgin and Kincardine, their Bruce kinsmen and in many civic arms of places associated with the Bruce.

So identified with the concept of Scotland was the emblem of its kings that the story is told of how an enraged **Edward** of England, laying siege to a Scots castle, demanded to know why it was held against him who had declared himself overlord of the Scots. The answer came that the fortress was held in the name of the King of Scots. Edward replied there was no longer any King of the Scots. The defenders defiantly rejoindered that they 'held of the Lion', the unquenchable symbol of their independence and identity as a nation.

Something of that same pride may have lead **James III** to enact in Parliament in 1471 that: 'in tyme to cum thar suld be na double tresor about his armys, bot that he suld ber hale armys of the lyoun without ony mare.' He may have intended by this to show that his sway as sovereign was not to be hedged in, but in fact it was but little observed. A few examples exist where the top of the tressure has been deleted but no more. It was closed again with the reign of James IV and the issue never reopened.

The King of Scots in battle array (Dennis).

From a drawing showing the achievement sent out from France with the arms of Mary as Queen of Scots quartered with those of her husband the Dauphin of France with an 'escutcheon of pretence' of the arms of England indicating expectation of succession-divided in two with a full second coat quartering Scotland and England thereby asserting Mary's status as Queen of England.

The royal arms of James III from the Trinity Altarpiece. The tressure is open across the top. The lion faces to the sinister toward the altar in the painting and wears a sort of extra-regal crown, never a formal feature of the arms (Burnett).

The lovely and tragic **Mary**, Queen of Scots from the age of six days, used heraldry as brilliant and confused as her own life. Married to the Dauphin of France, she quartered his arms with hers and, in her personal use, the arms of England as well to indicate her claim to that Crown. On the death of 'Bloody Mary' Tudor in 1558, the Scottish queen had indeed become the legitimate heir to the English throne in the eyes of the Catholic world, Elizabeth, daughter of Anne Boleyn and Henry VIII, being considered illegitimate. Mary, therefore, had a valid basis for her armorial claims, but they were to be used in evidence against her by the unforgiving Elizabeth when she finally had her tried and executed in 1587.

The royal arms of Scotland had been fixed for 400 years or more when, in 1603, Mary's son, James VI, was proclaimed King of England (and France) on the death of Elizabeth. The simple coat of arms of the King of Scots was then altered to incorporate his additional realms. It was the King's pleasure that his arms be *quartered*, that is, divided into four parts (below). In Scotland he had the rampant lion placed in the first and fourth quarters with the royal arms of England in the second quarter; this latter was already quartered with the fleurs-de-lys of France – in token of the old claim to the French throne – in its first and fourth quarters and the golden leopards of England in the junior second and third quarters. In the third quarter he introduced a golden harp for Ireland, the first time Ireland had been recognised in the arms of the Sovereign. In England, his

arms were to be marshalled with *England* (that is, France/England) in the first and fourth quarters, *Scotland* in the second and *Ireland* in the third – an effective and sensible arrangement which has generally been observed ever since. Similar adjustments had to be made in all the other components of the achievement, the total armorial composition, e.g. the supporters, crest and motto.

In 1426 James I had become the first King of Scots to use **supporters**, a unicorn in some instances and lions on his Privy Seal. Gradually the unicorn came to replace the lion supporters. James V, Mary and James VI used two unicorns with coronets at their necks and chains reflexed over their backs, supporting not only the shield and helm but also royal banners.

After 1603 James VI, now also James I of England, kept one of his **unicorns** and imported a lion supporter from the English royal arms. Again precedence was given to Scotland in Scotland, and the unicorn was not only placed on the right, dexter, or more honourable side, he was also given an Imperial Crown to match that worn by his lion counterpart. The unicorn supports a lance flying the saltire of St Andrew and the lion one with the red cross of St George for England. South of the border, however, pride of place was ceded to the lion, no banners are shown, and the Scots unicorn is not given a crown. Perhaps this is why 'The Lion and the Unicorn were fighting o'er the Crown'. It remains just so today.

Also dating from this union of the Crowns is the practice of displaying the Scottish Royal Crest, a red lion *sejant*

Illustration by the late Don Pottinger for a publication on the Battle of Bannockburn; the Lion and the Unicorn are evidently engaged in a 'full and frank exchange of views'.

Drawing of an illumination from a manuscript thought to predate 1454 and to have belonged to the Princess Eleanor, daughter of King James I and Queen Joan. It features a full achievement of Scotland with two unicorn supporters, gorged with simple coronets but without chains (Burnett).

Royal arms of William and Mary displaying the usual quartering but with King William's arms as Prince of Orange on an escutcheon. Ceremonial Burse of the Lord Chancellor of Scotland (Barden).

Royal arms of Queen Anne after the Union of 1707. The first and fourth quarters now impale the rampant lion of Scotland with the leopards of England in the manner of a marital union. A carved wooden panel from the Sovereign's Stall, the Thistle Chapel, High Kirk of St Giles, Edinburgh. By permission of the Minister of the High Kirk (Hodgson).

affronté (sitting, facing front), crowned and holding a sword in his right and a sceptre in his left paw, over the Crown and helm in Scotland rather than the English Royal Crest of a crowned golden lion standing upon the Crown. Likewise, the Scottish motto '*IN DEFENS*' – shortened from 'In my defense God me defend' – is used in place of '*Dieu et mon Droit*'. King James used a personal collar of thistles to encircle his shield. These days the shield will be encircled not with the Garter, as is done in England, but with the collar of the **Order of the Thistle** and will display its motto: '*Nemo me impune lacessit*', which may be translated formally as 'No one provokes me with impunity' and more bluntly as 'Waur daur meddle wi' me!'.

The Treaty of Union of 1707 dissolved the English and Scottish parliaments and replaced them with a single, new United Kingdom parliament. The treaty provided for **Queen Anne** to order her arms as she pleased to reflect the new union. She marshalled the arms as for a married couple, that is: the first and fourth quarters of the shield were now divided vertically and the rampant lion impaled in the dexter half in Scotland (but in the *sinister* or left side in England) with the leopards of England in the other. The wilted lilies of the tired claim to France were placed by themselves in the second quarter, and the harp left in the third.

With the accession of the House of **Hanover** to the throne, the arms of that kingdom were inserted in the fourth quarter. It was not until 1801 that King George III finally retired the lilies, gave Scotland and England their own quarters and placed Hanover on an escutcheon or small shield in the centre.

Royal arms of George IV or William IV showing the escutcheon of Hanover with a crown. This dates it neatly to between 1816, when Hanover became a kingdom, and 1837, when the crown of Hanover devolved on to her uncle the Duke of Cumberland on Victoria's accession to the throne. Carved wooden achievement behind the Lord President's chair in the First Division of the Inner House of the Court of Session, Parliament House, Edinburgh. By permission of the Lord President (Hodgson).

As can be traced in the marginal illustrations, there have been many other adjustments of the arms of the royal house reflecting the personal and political changes it has undergone, but the basic quartered format, shifting its order depending on which side of the border it is to be found, was established by James VI and I. As a woman, Queen Victoria could not succeed to the throne of Hanover which then devolved on an uncle, and its arms were removed. The royal arms have thus remained essentially unaltered since her ascension as a girl of 18 in 1837 amidst earnest and informed speculation she would be the last monarch of the British state.

THE LYON

The **Lyon** is Scotland's other king. From the late 13th century the Crown assumed control over the granting and marshalling of arms. The Sovereign as the fount of all honour remains the ultimate

The Lyon King of Arms with two of his heralds, Rothesay and Ross, and three pursuivants, Carrick, Kintyre and Unicorn. Note that the tabard of the Lord Lyon is velvet and cloth of gold, those of the heralds are embroidered on satin, and those of the pursuivants are of damask (Dennis).

OPPOSITE: *The heralds of Scotland at the opening of the Scottish parliament from a late 17th-century engraving in Nicolas Guendeville's* Atlas Historique. *Their pre-Union tabards bear only the lion rampant of Scotland (Burnett).*

authority in matters armorial. In Scotland, however, this power was delegated from a very early period exclusively to the Lyon King of Arms, the chief herald. He traces his office back beyond the dawn of heraldry to the ancient Celtic *Ard Sheanachidh*, the bard-recorder of the royal house, whose role merged with the analogous heraldic duties of the Lyon. His certificate of lineage was once required before the monarch could be crowned: at the Coronation in 1953, he was prepared to declaim, in Gaelic, Queen Elizabeth II's genealogy for the minimum seven generations or all the way back to the founder of the royal line, Fergus Mor MacErc in the fifth century – a process which reportedly took one and a half hours at the last purely Scottish coronation, that of Charles II in 1651.

The Lyon is one of the great officers of state, a judge over all matters armorial including the succession to titles and chiefships and name and change of name, in charge of all state, royal and public ceremonial in Scotland, and Controller of the Messengers at Arms. He is styled the Lord Lyon – Our Lyon to the Queen – and is entitled to the prefix 'The Right Honourable'. As the living symbol of sovereignty his person, like the monarch's, is sacred when in the discharge of his duties and to strike him is treason. Previously, he was actually crowned at his investiture by the king with the Crown of Scotland and is entitled to wear an unjewelled silver gilt version of the Scottish Crown. He is King of Arms and Secretary of the Most Ancient and Most Noble Order of the Thistle. His office predates his English counterpart, the Garter King of Arms. Unlike the English officers of arms who were established as a College of Heralds under the control of the Earl Marshal, the Duke of Norfolk, by King Richard III, the Lyon owns no superior other than his Sovereign. He and the other Scottish Officers of Arms remain an immediate part of Her Majesty's Household.

Heraldry is to be enjoyed and encouraged, but it must be done respecting its laws and traditions or it becomes a shambles and a mockery. The Lyon Court exists primarily to prevent such decadence. Its success has given Scots and Scotland the purest and most vigorous heraldic tradition in the world. Today the **Lyon Court** is primarily concerned with new grants of arms to

Disaster befell the Lyon Office in the loss of all its official records during the 17th century in the long upheavals of the Civil War, Cromwell's Commonwealth and the Restoration. There survive a handful of armorial works, examples from which illustrate this book. The Public Register of All Arms and Bearings in Scotland, still maintained today at the Lyon Court, dates from 1672. It was established by an act of the Scots parliament requiring all 'Prelates, Noblemen, Barons, and Gentlemen, who make vse of any Armes or Signes armoriall' to present proofs thereof to the Lyon Clerk within one year. The Lyon is there empowered to make grants of arms 'to vertuous and well-deserving Persones', but to impose a penalty of a £100 Scots per day, to seize all goods bearing unregistered arms and to remove illegal arms from any building of those who fail to comply. This is still the law.

THIS PAGE AND
OPPOSITE: *The Riding
of Parliament. Before
1707, members of the
Scottish parliament
marked the opening of
the session in Edinburgh
by riding from the Palace
of Holyroodhouse, up the
Royal Mile, to
Parliament Hall beside
the High Kirk of St
Giles. The Officers of
Arms took part in the
Riding of Parliament.*

individuals, companies and governmental offices and with matriculations, that is either recording the succession of the head of the family or issuing properly differenced arms to the junior members of armigerous families (in other words those already having duly recorded arms). As a **court of law** it has its Lyon Clerk and Keeper of the Records, a Procurator Fiscal and staff. The present Lyon Clerk and Keeper of the Records, also *Carrick Pursuivant*, is the first female officer of arms ever to have been appointed in the United Kingdom, a fact quite consistent with the equal status women have long enjoyed in Scots law. As a judge, the Lord Lyon sits formally in his Household uniform and ermine furred crimson judicial robe to hear contested proofs – the direct successor to that red-robed High Sennachie who is recorded officiating at the coronation of Alexander III in 1249. More often, however, petitions are processed routinely in a very much more mundane manner.

In addition to the Lord Lyon and his staff, the Court of the Lord Lyon is also comprised of 'his brether Herauldis'. Originally six **heralds** and six **pursuivants**, their number was halved in 1867. Appointed by the Lyon, they accompany him on State occasions, present petitions and appear before him as officers of his Court. Their titles, assigned now in rotation, are ancient and evocative: the heralds Albany, Islay, Marchmont, Ross, Rothesay and Snowdoun, the pursuivants Bute, Carrick, Dingwall, Kintyre, Ormonde and Unicorn. There are other ancient titles, too, Falkland, Linlithgow and March, which now are used only rarely when appointing pursuivants extraordinary for a special purpose. Clad in the gorgeous state

tabards, holding their batons of office, they add rich colour and solemn dignity to state occasions and visibly embody the sovereign and ancient realm of Scotland.

Quite apart from the Officers of Arms of the Royal Household, Scotland enjoys a number of private pursuivants still attached to great houses from long centuries past: **Slains** for the Earls of Erroll, Lord High Constables of Scotland, **Garioch** for the Earldom of Mar and **Endure** for the Earls of Crawford.

THE CROWN OF SCOTLAND

The Crown of Scotland together with the sword of state and sceptre form the **Honours of Scotland**, the crown jewels of the realm and the oldest regalia in the United Kingdom. Incorporating the materials of the earlier crown, the Crown was reworked for James V in 1540. It varies substantially from the present Crown of St Edward made for Charles II's coronation as King of England in 1661 and used thereafter at coronations in England. The old English regalia had been callously destroyed by order of Parliament. Charles had, in fact, been hastily crowned King of Scots at Scone on New Year's Day 1651 before being forced to flee in advance of the Parliamentary forces sent hurrying North by Cromwell to punish the Scots for acknowledging their king. It was the last time the Crown of Scotland was used for a coronation. The heroic defence and rescue of the Honours of Scotland from Cromwell's determined troops is a bright episode in a confused time. Hardly less curious, however, has been their subsequent fate.

A stylised version of the Crown of Scotland used by the Post Office in Scotland (Burnett).

The Crown of Scotland, remodelled for James V in 1540, is the oldest royal crown in the United Kingdom (Historic Scotland).

They were returned from their hiding place under the floor of Kinneff Kirk at the Restoration and used again at all sessions of the Scottish parliament, the symbol of the king in parliament. At each sitting they were removed with great ceremony from Edinburgh Castle and brought to Parliament Hall in the dramatic procession known as the Riding of the Parliament then laid on a table before the throne while parliament was in session. A bill became law when the sceptre was lifted and touched to it in token of the Royal Consent.

The last act it touched was the Treaty of Union which expressly provided for the Honours to stay in Scotland:' and that they shall so remain in all times coming, notwithstanding the Union'. In fact they were put in a great chest, walled up in the Crown Room of Edinburgh Castle and all but forgotten. One hundred and eleven years later their sleep was disturbed by anxious Officers of State and Walter Scott armed with a Royal Warrant to rediscover them. Since then they have been on public display, ready to fulfil any further role the future might hold for them.

It is gratifying to note that the Crown of Scotland can, indeed, be

A heraldic version of the English crown, the St Edward's Crown which is kept in the Tower of London (Burnett) and left, the crown itself (Crown copyright, reproduced by permission of the Controller of HMSO).

seen on increasingly public display. Observe the heraldic representations in the margin: the familiar Imperial Crown, obviously derived from St Edward's Crown and that taken from the Crown of Scotland. A careful eye will see this latter form in regular and appropriate use throughout the land. The Lyon Office must be thanked for its contribution to the careful fostering of the nation's symbols.

CHAPTER 4

ARCHITECTURAL ENHANCEMENT

Having looked at the rules which govern the 'gentle science', their application in the descent of arms and their flamboyant flowering in the royal arms, we now begin to look more widely at heraldry in action.

From early in its inception, heraldry was universally exploited for its practical and decorative qualities. In this chapter we highlight one of its most visible applications – as the external adornment for a whole range of buildings and their settings.

Carved heraldry in stone is the most public source for appreciating the impact of armory on the architectural heritage of Scotland. On buildings, large areas of wall surface were punctured by judicious use of window spacing and simple mouldings defined doorways and floor levels. Carved decoration in the form of heraldic panels added emphasis initially around doorways but as time passed these began to be placed higher up until they reached the roofline. There they took up position amongst chimneys, dormer windows, gables and pepperpot towers. The importance of heraldic display was not confined to exterior use and we shall see in the next chapters how interiors and furnishings were also subject to this form of enhancement.

From 1500 until 1850 heraldry on buildings usually indicated ownership either by the Crown or an individual. During the second half of the 19th century the vast building programme of civic architecture with new municipal buildings, churches, art galleries, museums and specialist industrial buildings saw a revival in decorative heraldry in order to symbolise civic or patriotic pride, or corporate ownership. Glasgow, Aberdeen, Greenock, Hawick and other burghs erected municipal chambers, blazoned with civic arms; Dundee and Glasgow built the Albert Institute and Kelvingrove Museum and Art Gallery, each embellished with armorial display, but overshadowing all is the remarkable **Scottish National Portrait Gallery** in

OPPOSITE: *Royal arms of James VI flanked by the arms of the Earl of Mar and his wife Annabella Murray of Tullibardine decorating Mar's Wark, Stirling (Historic Scotland).*

Edinburgh where a unified heraldic scheme covers both exterior and interior. Over 120 coats of arms rendered in stone, paint and stained glass record individuals, institutions and societies which formed the colourful historic structure of Scotland.

The sacrifice of thousands of Scottish men and women in the conflict of the First World War is remembered in the **Scottish National War Memorial** within Edinburgh Castle (left) and on numerous war memorials throughout Scotland. Heraldry is used in the National War Memorial and on many local memorials, such as that in Aberdeen, to symbolise the local areas which suffered unforgettable loss.

THE DISPLAY OF ROYAL ARMS

The **royal arms** of Scotland or of the United Kingdom are seen on a variety of buildings. Why this is so varies. With the introduction of the feudal system most great landowners held their estates directly from the King of Scots. Landowners placed the royal arms over their own arms at the main entrance to castles and tower-houses to

At Tolquhon Castle, Aberdeenshire, the royal arms appear above those of the owner, William Forbes of Tolquhon (Historic Scotland).

demonstrate this link with the Crown. Examples are numerous: Huntly Castle (below) and Tolquhon Castle, also in Aberdeenshire, emphasise the importance of the combination by mounting the arms between flanking towers and there are many abandoned tower-houses with fine moulded, but now empty, housings which once held personal and royal arms.

The links between **Crown** and **Church** are demonstrated heraldically at Spynie Palace in Moray, once the seat of the powerful Bishops of Moray whose *Cathedra* in Elgin also carries regal armory on the pillar which supports the Chapter House vault. Seton Collegiate Church in East Lothian bears an example of the post-1471 Act of Parliament royal arms as does the High Kirk of St Giles in Edinburgh, though the latter example has been altered at a later date. Royal buildings inhabited by succeeding monarchs naturally carry the devices of the King of Scots. The Palaces of Linlithgow, Falkland and Holyroodhouse provide a variety of carved examples, some of which are later replacements. At Edinburgh and Stirling castles there are the empty housings which once contained arms

By displaying certain arms, religious belief can be made public. The most spectacular example of this is the great heraldic table above the main entrance to Huntly Castle, Aberdeenshire. Erected in 1602 by George Gordon, 1st Marquess of Huntly, it consists of personal heraldry, the royal arms, the attributed arms of Jesus Christ (the Arma Christi), an inscribed panel stating in Latin, 'It is not fitting that we glory in anything but the Cross of our Lord Jesus Christ', a roundel carved with the head of Christ surrounded by a sunburst, and finally the figure of St Michael the Archangel. George Gordon was a staunch Catholic and despite the Reformation, he was undaunted in openly proclaiming his beliefs. The carvings were defaced by religious zealots in 1651.

The great heraldic frontispiece at Huntly Castle, Aberdeenshire, of 1602 with a hierarchical progression of armory which reads from bottom to top (Historic Scotland).

A combination of royal and episcopal heraldry grouped together at Spynie Palace, near Elgin, residence of the Bishops of Moray (Historic Scotland).

destroyed by Cromwell's soldiers in 1651.

One known stone carver, William Wallace, was particularly fond of employing armorial detail. Part of the palace block in Edinburgh Castle was remodelled between 1615 and 1617 by Wallace prior to James VI's one and only return visit to Scotland after becoming King of England. The carver used **royal emblems** on the pediments above each window to symbolise the Union of the Crowns. Thistles, roses, crowns, a portcullis, a harp, along with the king's cipher and the date 1616 are featured. William Wallace repeated this decorative approach two years later at Linlithgow Palace where he had to rebuild the west range. There the window pediments again have Union symbolism with additional devices associated with the title of Prince of Wales. The unexpected death of Prince Henry in 1612 had caused his younger brother, Charles, to become heir with the titles Duke of Rothesay and Prince of Wales. Linlithgow bears thistles, fleurs-de-lys, roses, the crest lion of Scotland and the cipher and three feathers of Charles, Prince of Wales.

The unique double-sided finial of the Mercat Cross, Fraserburgh, Aberdeenshire, showing the royal arms of Scotland and the arms of Great Britain, c.1606 (Burnett).

Royal proclamations were made throughout Scotland at the **mercat** (market) **cross** of each royal burgh. Many of these crosses still survive and carry the symbols of royal authority. Aberdeen possesses the finest extant cross and although it dates from 1686 when regular royal proclamations had ceased throughout Scotland, the royal arms are part of the decorative scheme. The burgh of Inverkeithing in Fife has a shaft cross with royal and Douglas heraldry, and the Victorian replacement mercat cross of 1885 in Edinburgh carries both the royal arms of Scotland and of the United Kingdom plus six other shields all bright with heraldic colour. An unusual double Scottish/United Kingdom cross is located at Fraserburgh, Aberdeenshire, dating from soon after 1603. This was recently restored and re-tinctured.

Buildings erected by government acting on behalf of the Crown mainly date from the early 18th century onward. Most are identified by a carved version of the royal arms of the United Kingdom in use at the time of building, so that the development of these arms can be studied and employed to date the particular building. Several structures were erected after Mrs Coade of London had invented the artificial stone to which she gave her name. Coade stone was modelled or cast from moulds before firing at a high temperature to produce architectural features which architects could incorporate into their buildings. There are Coade stone royal arms above the main entrance to Fort George near Inverness and at the former Bridge of Don Barracks in Aberdeen, both painted in heraldic colours.

Apart from military installations, new **custom houses** were required in Leith, Glasgow, and later in Dundee. These are in a neo-classical style, Leith and Dundee having pillars and a pediment filled

Royal arms of the United Kingdom from the reign of King George II modelled in Coade stone at Fort George, Ardesier, Inverness-shire (Historic Scotland).

Central pediment of Leith Custom House housing the wooden royal arms carved by John Steele in 1813 (Burnett).

Modern carved stone royal arms of the United Kingdom as used in Scotland; St Andrew's House, Edinburgh, 1938 (Historic Scotland).

with a fully carved version of the royal arms. There was a spate of new **Post Office** buildings constructed under the short reign of King Edward VII and the early part of his successor King George V. Aberdeen has a grand granite baronial edifice; other buildings were more modest such as the post offices in Banff, Musselburgh and Galashiels but each carries either the royal arms or the King's cipher. The now-demolished Labour Exchange at Tollcross in Edinburgh (1913) was another type of government office which bore carved royal arms. These were fortunately saved and are now in the collection of the National Museums of Scotland.

The finest example of carved royal arms of the United Kingdom, as used in Scotland, from more recent times was created by the

Musselburgh-born sculptor Alexander Carrick (1882–1966). The arms were executed for St Andrew's House, Calton Hill, Edinburgh, formerly the main seat of government in Scotland. The building was completed in 1939 just before the outbreak of the Second World War and Carrick's superb carving amply demonstrates how heraldry can be used for decorative emphasis at a main entrance whilst proclaiming the Crown purpose of the building.

PERSONAL ARMS

Personal arms are a feature of 16th- and 17th-century tower-houses and funeral monuments. Aberdeenshire is particularly rich in both, often found in unexpected places. One unusual location is the **Wine Tower** at Fraserburgh. This is a simple three-storey structure beside Kinnaird Head Lighthouse, with an upper room once used as a private chapel by Sir Alexander Fraser of Philorth. The room is decorated with a series of seven hanging roof bosses; three occupy the centre of the roof vault, the remaining four being located in window alcoves. All are carved in the round but the central three are most original in concept. Each is a complete coat of arms with all, or some, of the usual elements – shield, helmet, crest, motto and supporters. They portray the *Arma Christi,* the royal arms and the arms of Sir Alexander Fraser of Philorth. The three bosses are unlike any other found in Scotland and constitute the finest carved heraldry of the late 16th century. The four window bosses are more conventional and bear a series of carved shields showing ancestral heraldry of the Frasers.

The arms of William Duff of Braco on the south front of Duff House, Banff.

Exploded drawing of the roof pendant from the Wine Tower, Fraserburgh, Aberdeenshire, bearing the arms of Sir Alexander Fraser of Philworth, post 1570 (John Borland for Banff & Buchan District Council).

There are over 600 castles and tower-houses in Scotland scattered from the border in the south to Orkney in the north. Most can be found along the eastern side of the country concentrated in areas with associated good farm land. Not all are inhabited or display the arms of owners but in Fife, Angus, and Aberdeenshire there are many which do sport personal heraldry.

Once the requirement for defence had been superseded by the desire for more gracious homes, the **country house** became a feature of the Scottish landscape. Some are on a grand scale like Drumlanrig Castle, Ayrshire (finished 1697) Hopetoun House, West Lothian (finished 1746) and the uncompleted Duff House in Banff (main block finished 1760) but most are more modest. Several bear the personal heraldry of the builder adapted for inclusion in a baroque or neo-classical style. Drumlanrig and Duff have heraldic pediments; however, apart from the pediments, classical architecture does not provide as sympathetic a setting for heraldic symbols as does the Gothic style.

Old **graveyards** and cemeteries are a rich source of personal armory. The Howff in Dundee and the old graveyard in Banff are worthy of study, though the finest concentration of heraldic monuments is in Greyfriars Churchyard, Edinburgh. This was established in 1562, extended in 1636, 1703, and finally in 1798. The range of tomb type is large and shows how funerary taste altered over the centuries.

The second half of the 19th century was a period of multistyle architecture including new interest in Scotland's native building traditions which resulted in the **Scottish Baronial style**. Once again heraldry came into its own through the detailed study by R W Billings, author of *Baronial and Ecclesiastical Antiquities of Scotland* (1845–1852), and the systematic research of David MacGibbon and Thomas Ross which revealed the wealth of Scotland's inherited architecture. They published a five-volume work entitled *The Castellated and Domestic Architecture of Scotland* between 1887 and 1892, and followed this in 1896 with three volumes covering *The Ecclesiastical Architecture of Scotland*.

These volumes inspired a generation of native architects; two in particular fully exploited the decorative effect of armory: Sir Robert Rowand Anderson (1835–1920),

Carved achievement of the Earl of Leven and Melville adjacent to the entrance of the Thistle Chapel, High Kirk of St Giles, Edinburgh. The Leven and Melville family provided the money to build the chapel (Hodgson).

and Sir Robert Lorimer (1864–1929). Of all the churches, educational buildings and houses Anderson created two are especially rich in symbolic and heraldic detail. Mount Stuart, commissioned by John, 3rd Marquess of Bute and designed in 1879, makes full use of Crichton-Stuart heraldry. The year 1891 saw the opening of the Scottish National Portrait Gallery, already mentioned, in which Anderson turned the history of Scotland literally to stone by lavish use of heraldry and sculpture. In a similar way Lorimer also produced two key buildings which heavily rely on heraldry for decorative effect: the Chapel of the Most Ancient and Most Noble Order of the Thistle, built adjacent to the High Kirk of St Giles in 1911 and the Scottish National War Memorial, completed in 1927.

Marriage stone of Sir William Gray of Pittendrum and his wife, Geile Smith of Grothill, the original owners of the building now known as Lady Stair's House in Edinburgh.

MARRIAGE STONES

Marriage stones provide a further vehicle for heraldic display which is both personal and practical. The stereotypical 'dour Scot' could demonstrate a romantic streak in his nature by the visible record of a marriage above the main door of the marital home. The stone lintel carried the initials of husband and wife together with the date of building the home, or the year of their marriage. Thus the stone was also the solid recording of their alliance. Often an appropriate text from scripture would also be carved, such as 'UNLESS THE LORD BUILDS' or 'BLESSIT BE THIS HOUSE'. If husband and wife were in right of arms, then an impaled version of both arms are found on the marriage stone.

An extension of the practice is sometimes seen on the pediments of dormer windows where a combined monogram was located. (Fine examples from the Palace at Culross in Fife are illustrated in Beaton's *Scotland's Traditional Houses* in this series.) There are smaller Scottish houses with initials and dates carved on skewputs, the terminal stones at each end of a building between wall head and gable.

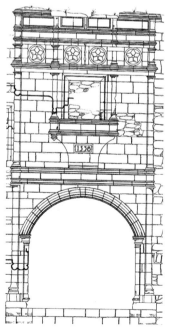

The entrance to the castle at St Andrews bearing four cinquefoils from the arms of the archbishop, John Hamilton. The empty panel below once held a carving of the archbishop's arms.

These features demonstrate how essential it is while looking at an example of Scottish architecture to gaze upwards so as not to miss the many small details of interest to be found at rooftop level.

ARMS AS DECORATION

Decorative detail in architecture was often drawn from the main elements in a coat of arms.

The original doorway to the Hamilton Dower House, Prestonpans, East Lothian, with cinquefoils used as decoration on either side of the shield within the pediment.

an earlier example dating from 1577 is in Edinburgh Castle where the Portcullis Gate is surmounted by an heraldic panel within a classical-style frame. The frame is decorated with silver stars and red hearts – charges from the arms of James Douglas, 4th Earl of Morton, who was Regent of Scotland at the time the Gate was erected.

At the Hamilton Dower House in Prestonpans, East Lothian (1628), the **cinquefoil** charge associated with Hamilton armory is used as a finial on two dormer windows and on the pediment above the main entrance. The Hamilton cinquefoil had been used the previous century as a decorative device on the Fore Tower of St Andrews Castle, a fortification rebuilt by Archbishop John Hamilton *c.* 1555, some 20 years before the Douglas charges appeared on the Portcullis Gate at Edinburgh Castle.

All these examples are located in central Scotland but heraldic detailing can be seen in many other areas of the kingdom as an indication of how widespread this imaginative practice spread amongst Scottish masons.

Heraldic display in the gardens at Edzell Castle, Angus: LEFT: *general view of the pleasance showing part of the chequered boundary wall;* RIGHT: *impaled arms of the husband and wife who added the pleasance to Edzell Castle (Historic Scotland).*

HERALDRY IN THE GARDEN

Gardens were not ignored by owners wishing to make their heraldic mark. Edzell Castle in Angus provides the most outstanding heraldic garden setting in Scotland. The castle and adjoining Pleasance were created by a cadet branch of the Lindsay family. The main charge of their arms is a *fess chequy*, like the diced band on a policeman's cap. The internal surface of the garden wall is pierced with a series of *chequer-board* holes intended as flower boxes. One can imagine the wall filled with alternate blue and white flowers to reflect the heraldic tinctures. The garden contains a carved stone panel bearing the combined arms of Sir David Lindsay of Edzell and his wife Dame Isobel Forbes, the creators of the castle and garden.

Edzell Pleasance is an unique creation in Scotland but other gardens have items of heraldic interest. Pinkie House, Musselburgh, has an elaborate well head carrying the arms and monogram of the owner, Alexander Seton, first Earl of Dunfermline. He was one of the outstanding heraldic patrons during the reign of James VI and I, responsible for the great facade at Fyvie Castle, Aberdeenshire, and for heraldic decoration executed in both paint and plaster inside

Design for the heraldic parterre at Pitmedden Garden, Aberdeenshire, showing the arms of Sir Alexander Seton of Pitmedden (National Trust for Scotland).

Pinkie House. In the grounds of Dundas Castle, West Lothian, there is a remarkable fountain **sundial**, dating from 1623, which was made for Sir Walter Dundas and his wife Dame Ann Menteith. It is highly ornamented and amongst the swirls and flourishes can be found the Dundas crest, the Dundas rampant lion and the quartered arms of Dundas and Menteith coupled with the salamander badge of the house of Dundas.

A modern heraldic garden scheme was created several years ago by the National Trust of Scotland at **Pitmedden Garden**, Aberdeenshire. One of the *parterres* (formal beds) is laid out with a central heraldic panel of Sir Alexander Seton, first owner of Pitmedden, flanked by saltires and thistle emblems, all rendered in heraldic tinctures with flowers of the appropriate colours.

Thus armory has provided decorative interest to the exterior of many buildings in several ways and by looking inside several Scottish houses the heraldic hunter will discover a continuity of armorial usage.

CHAPTER 5

FLOWERY FURNISHING

The Scottish interior provides a rich array of surfaces and spaces for the exploitation of heraldry. Over the centuries a number of specific locations became popular for the display of armory, in particular ceilings, fireplaces, and a range of furnishings. Taking each in turn, this chapter features significant examples that indicate the enormous variety that still survive.

OPPOSITE: *Embroidered wall-hanging from the late 17th century, featuring the armorial achievement of Hume of Whitfield (Burnett).*

CEILINGS

Many medieval castle and church ceilings were originally vaulted stone as in the great vault with painted heraldry at Balbegno Castle. By the 15th and 16th centuries, native and imported timber was used

Interior of St Machar's Cathedral, Old Aberdeen, showing the granite nave with the wooden heraldic ceiling of 1520 (Burnett).

Arms of Pope Leo X, fixed to the ceiling of St Machar's Cathedral, high above the Holy Table (Burnett).

to make flat wooden ceilings. Important buildings such as churches and royal residences had applied decoration fixed to the ceilings, smaller domestic ceilings were painted with tempera colour. The earliest example of imaginative roof display is in **St Machar's Cathedral**, Old Aberdeen. The nave of the granite cathedral is roofed over with a flat wooden cover, divided into squares by raised mouldings which have three rows of 16 carved and painted shields fixed at their intersections. These record the political states of Europe, the ecclesiastical dignities of Scotland, and the king and nobles of Scotland around 1520 when the ceiling was completed. The 48 armorial devices constitute a unique record of the time and have no parallel in the United Kingdom.

At the Palace of **Holyroodhouse** in Edinburgh, the north-west tower, built for James V between 1528 and 1532, contains a compartmented wooden ceiling in the room known as Mary Queen of Scots' outer chamber. This ceiling carries roundels with the arms of Mary, her father, James V, her father-in-law, Henry II and her first husband, Franşçois II, as Dauphin of France. These may have been added 30 years after her death in 1617. Later the same type of compartmented wooden ceiling is found at Falkland Palace, decorated in 1633 with the royal emblems and initials of Charles I, his Queen, Henrietta Maria, and their son Charles, Duke of Rothesay and Prince of Wales.

The flat wooden compartmented ceiling was revived during the 19th century in Scotland and a good example is found once again in Aberdeen. The former council chamber in the Municipal Building of 1871 has an heraldic ceiling erected in 1877 with 84 shields representing people and institutions with significance to Aberdeen. Another is to be seen in the old Council Chambers in Leith.

In smaller domestic interiors of the late 16th and early 17th centuries ceilings consisted of *beams* with *boards* laid on top at right angles. The boards formed the floor of the room above. The beams and underside of the boards were decorated with tempera colour which have given Scotland a unique collection some of which were long hidden under later lath and plaster additions. Many painted schemes involve heraldry, either as an adjunct to a theme of decoration, or as the main subject. At Earlshall Castle in Fife the main hall has a flat-vaulted ceiling painted in monochrome with a pattern of linked circles and rectangles. The circles contain 72 armorial achievements from both Scotland and overseas. The rectangles form frames for representations of 105 real and fabulous animals. Shields of arms are also painted at Crathes Castle, at Nunraw House in Lothian, and on two ceilings at Collarnie Castle in Fife, though the latter are in a perilous state.

Soon after the Union of the Crowns in 1603 a new fashion in interior decoration was introduced to Scotland, namely ornamental plasterwork. Groups of itinerant craftsmen entered Scotland bringing with them their wooden moulds. Use of the moulds to cast decorative plaster details gives evidence that these men worked their way up the east coast, plastering a number of houses such as Pinkie in Musselburgh, Balcarres in Fife, Glamis Castle in Angus, Muchalls

The monochrome painted tempera ceiling in the Great Hall, Earlshall, Fife (Historic Scotland).

Castle in Kincardineshire and Craigievar Castle in Aberdeenshire. In all of these houses either the royal arms or the personal armory of the owner was modelled or cast in plaster.

PANELLING

While timber was always used for ceilings in the late Middle Ages, bare stone walls began to be covered with wooden panelling as well to provide greater warmth and comfort. A few surviving examples show that some panelling was highly decorative. Fragments dating from the 1530s, exhibited in the Royal Museum of Scotland, were commissioned by David Beaton, later Cardinal and Archbishop of St Andrews. As well as two panels of religious significance there is an excellent *Arma Christi*, the royal arms of Scotland and a composite panel of carved arms belonging to the family of the cardinal. Also in the National Museums collection is

The most elaborate version of the Arma Christi extant in Scotland carved on the Beaton Panels, c. 1520 in the National Museums, Edinburgh (Burnett).

another section of woodwork known as the *Killochan Panels*, dated 1606. They are a combination of foreign and native craftsmanship and bear the arms of John Cathcart and his wife Helen Wallace. The panels were made for their home, Killochan Castle near Dumfries.

THE FIREPLACE

The fireplace is the central feature of any home, a focus as much

Portraits of the owner and his lady over the bedroom fireplace at Huntly Castle (Historic Scotland).

of display as warmth, be it in castle or cottage. In grand homes the surround to the fire was often a location for armorial flourish. *Huntly Castle* contains two stone-carved fireplaces, one in a principal chamber, the other in a private family room. The former carries the royal arms of Great Britain accompanied by the impaled achievement of George, first Marquess of Huntly, and his wife Henrietta Stewart, daughter of the Duke of Lennox, all set within an elaborate framework. The fireplace is dated 1606. The second fireplace is not so imposing but has an intimate charm as it carries two portrait roundels. As these flank the arms of the marquess and marchioness, the roundels probably represent the builder of Huntly Castle and his spouse. The expense of carved stone at Huntly can be compared to the less expensive plaster fireplace decoration at Craigievar and Muchalls castles where giant versions of the royal arms have been placed above the great hall fireplace.

Elaborate fireplace at Huntly Castle, with the arms of the owner the Marquess of Huntly, and his sovereign, James VI and I (Historic Scotland).

Carvings on fireplace lintels were quite small in the medieval period, and these examples from the 17th century represent the culmination of this practise.

FURNITURE AND FURNISHINGS

Furnishings, the additional features of any home which provide comfort or convenience, were sparse in Scotland during the medieval period. Initially **chairs** and canopied **beds** were luxuries restricted to a privileged group, as is demonstrated by the chairs of Alexander Burnett of Leys and his wife. Burnett and his wife also commissioned a magnificent carved bed in 1594, so constructed that they could lie in it and look up at a carved roof, or tester, bearing their impaled arms, combined monogram, and portraits.

One group of Scots who could afford more expensive furnishings were guild craftsmen who formed a powerful elite in the administration of Scottish burghs. They controlled trade practices and the quality of goods which gave them outstanding corporate status.

In an age before the mass production of furniture, individual chairs were a mark of status. A fine example of this is the pair of chairs in Crathes Castle, Kincardineshire, made for Alexander Burnett of Leys and his wife Katherine Gordon in 1597. Each chair is identified by the arms of the user (Burnett).

Their civic standing was reflected in the aura surrounding the head of the guild, be he master or deacon. The deacon's chair was like a mini-throne and there is an excellent collection of guild chairs in the hall of the Incorporated Trades of Aberdeen, better known locally as Trinity Hall. Many of the chairs carry the arms of the guild or the personal arms of the deacon who donated the chair. Another group of typical Scottish chairs, some heraldic, is to be found in Provand's Lordship, Glasgow's oldest secular building, adjacent to Glasgow Cathedral. These have been gathered together from various parts of Scotland and constitute the largest collection of native furniture of the 16th and 17th centuries.

Several Scottish kirks contain the **pews** of individuals or corporate bodies such as the trade guilds. They display the armorial ensigns of those who had the right to sit there. One of the most elaborate examples is to be found in Kilbirnie Kirk, Ayrshire, where the local laird, John, first Viscount Garnock, embellished the family pew in 1705 with his own arms and 17 other shields with arms of his ancestors.

*The Crawford Aisle,
Kilbirnie Auld Kirk,
Ayrshire, embellished
with family armory in
1705 by the First
Viscount Garnock
(Jones).*

During the 17th century it was fashionable to cover dining tables with specially woven **carpets**. Sometimes these carried armory or appropriate personal symbols. The Lyon family had such a carpet bearing the coronet and cypher of the Earls of Strathmore at Glamis Castle. This is now in the collection of the National Museums of Scotland in Edinburgh but there is an even more elaborate carpet still in private hands at Arniston House, south of Edinburgh. Although the carpet has been cut in half and reduced in length there is sufficient remaining to indicate how impressive it must have been when first embroidered by Katharine Oliphant around 1590. She signed the work with her initials and placed her arms in the middle of the composition, two oval figurative panels devoted to wine and food, linked by flowers and foliaceous ornament within a continuous border of flowers and birds. Sadly, besides the fine example on the frontispiece to this chapter, there are few other early examples of embroidery left in Scotland although England possesses a collection of panels worked by Mary Queen of Scots during her long imprisonment there. Many of these use pseudo-heraldic motifs as the main decorative element.

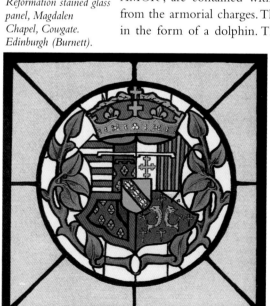

FIXTURES AND FITTINGS

Apart from furniture and soft furnishings, heraldry also appears in the work of blacksmiths. In the days before electric door bells, house visitors in Scotland used a **knocker** to announce their arrival at the front door. Fyvie Castle in Aberdeenshire, now a National Trust for Scotland property, once had a metal door knocker, the handle of which carried the arms of Alexander Seton, Lord Fyvie with his motto engraved vertically above. The knocker plate extended the heraldic scheme by having an elaborate outline composed of crescents and fleurs-de-lys, components of the arms. A more sophisticated door knocker is to be found at Muness Castle in Shetland. This has been conceived as a piece of three-dimensional design to be viewed from both front and side. It bears a shield of arms, helmet with flowing mantling and crest. The owner's name, 'ANDRO BRVS' (Andrew Bruce), and motto, '*OMNIA FINCIT AMOR*', are contained within the shield area without detracting from the armorial charges. The knocker itself, seen from the side, is in the form of a dolphin. The composition and execution in cast bronze are skilfully done and could have been imported from Scandinavia or the Low Countries, which might account for the transliteration of 'VINCIT' – of Love *conquers* all – to 'FINCIT'.

Cast bronze heraldic door knocker from Muness Castle, Unst, Shetland (Burnett).

The arms of Mary of Guise and Lorraine, second wife of James V featured in a pre-Reformation stained glass panel, Magdalen Chapel, Cowgate. Edinburgh (Burnett).

HERALDRY ON GLASS

One other element of furnishing which added to comfort in the later medieval period was glazing. Although **stained glass** was used in ecclesiastical buildings such as the Magdalen Chapel in Edinburgh, erected in the reign of James V, and containing the only extant

Panel of the Royal Arms of Scotland from the great window of Parliament Hall, commemorating the founding of the College of Justice by James V in 1532. The window was installed in 1867 (Hodgson).

pre-Reformation glass to be found in Scotland (consisting of four armorial roundels within a floral frame), early secular glass is rarer still. Fyvie Castle contains a stained-glass heraldic roundel, dated 1599, which carries the arms of Alexander Seton as Lord Fyvie.

Heraldic glass on a grand scale did not appear in Scotland until the second half of the 19th century. Edinburgh and Glasgow house splendid examples particularly in the Parliament Hall and Glasgow Cathedral but Aberdeen boasts the finest example in the **Mitchell Hall**, Marischal College, Aberdeen's second university, which was amalgamated with King's College in 1860.

Heraldry in action: segment of the stunning heraldic display on the Great Window of the Mitchell Hall, Marischal College, Aberdeen (University of Aberdeen). Its design, researched by University Librarian P J Anderson, summarised in pictorial form the history of the University and included elements of the 17th-century heraldic ceiling of old Marischal College. This section shows top, shields of the first eight principals, portraits including the founder George, 4th Earl Marischal, and below, shields of ten early benefactors.

CHAPTER 6

A DIGNIFIED END

We have seen heraldic display in operation both within and without Scotland's great houses. In this final chapter one other major aspect of its use is explored: its application to those elements that mark the end of the armiger's life, the funeral hatchment, the coffin and the tomb.

The funeral hatchment of General Fraser, 16th Lord Saltoun KT, GCB, GCH, in St Peter's Episcopal Church, Fraserburgh, 1853 (Burnett).

Funerals still retain a degree of sombre formality but it is only a shadow of the panoply of death regularly organised in Scotland during the 17th century. Because heraldry reflects status, any honour due to a deceased person could be demonstrated publicly with an array of armorial display at their funeral. The Scottish Officers of Arms became involved to ensure accurate coats of arms were on show, and naturally fees were claimed by them for their services!

In one way possession of a coat of arms is the nearest thing to immortality to be sustained in this life as the arms are passed from one generation to another in the direct line of descent. Heraldry at a funeral was therefore also an indication of continuity, linking the past with the future.

Scots are a sentimental people, and in the 17th century part of the armorial display at a funeral contained symbolic signs of grief in the form of tear drops. Banners decorated with a winged hour-glass or a skull and bones reminded onlookers of their own inevitable end, but family pride would be demonstrated by an array of probative heraldry to show the descent of the deceased. Funeral palls were covered with escutcheons of arms, the initials of the individual concerned, and with an array of paper or canvas tear shapes pinned on to the pall.

Heraldic funeral flags carried at the funeral of the Duke of Rothes, 1681.

Pall-covered coffin and canopy, Rothes funeral 1681.

An engraved record of the obsequies arranged for the funeral of John, Duke of Rothes, which took place in Edinburgh on 23rd August 1681, shows the array of heraldic content present on such an occasion. Eighty-three banners and 51 painted coats of arms were prepared by heraldic painters for the highly symbolic decoration of the cortege. Over 243 individuals took part in the procession. All this was intended to reinforce the status and familial descent of Scotland's Lord High Chancellor. This was the most elaborate funeral procession ever seen on the streets of Edinburgh, but from the evidence of the surviving funeral accounts, less influential mortals of the landed classes also marked their passing with varying degrees of similar heraldic display.

The Lord Lyon King of Arms carrying the hatchment of the Duke of Rothes at his funeral of 1681.

FUNERAL HATCHMENTS

One piece of heraldry carried in the procession was a diamond–shaped board painted with the arms of the deceased. A descriptive word for a coat of arms with all its surrounding features is, as we saw in Chapter 1, an 'achievement'; from this term is derived the word *hatchment*, the name eventually applied to this diamond-shaped board. In time, two hatchments were painted, but not for carrying in the procession. One was hung above the main door of the deceased's home and the other was displayed at the place of interment; often this would be inside the family vault.

The hatchment was a feature common to Scottish, English and North European funeral practice, and as the centuries passed funerals became less elaborate but the hatchment was retained as the last residual reminder of former heraldic extravagance.

The funeral hatchment of John, 1st Duke of Atholl, d. 1724 (Nisbet).

Scotland has over 50 surviving funeral hatchments – many less than England – which are scattered across the country. There are two concentrated collections: at **Luss Parish Kirk** beside Loch Lomond, commemorating members of the Colquhoun of Luss family, and at **Weem Old Kirk** in Perthshire which is the burial place of the Menzies of that Ilk.

The Scottish hatchment differed from those found in England. The dead person's coat of arms was surrounded with smaller ancestral shields; in each corner of the hatchment there was a **skull** with **crossed bones** underneath, and the intervening spaces were painted with symbolic tears. A good example of the old-style funeral hatchment is hung in the office of the Lord Lyon King of Arms within New Register House in Edinburgh.

After the Treaty of Union with England in 1707, influences from the south became more apparent, even in the painting of hatchments which followed the less elaborate English style. Yet even now, hatchments have not gone completely out of fashion: this most public form of heraldic display was last seen in Edinburgh during 1988 at Arthur Lodge to mark the passing of J Pinkerton Esquire.

A recent hatchment seen in Edinburgh during 1988 commemorating John Pinkerton QC (Burnett).

Lead outer coffin of Sir Robert Montgomerie, d. 1651, in the Skelmorlie Aisle, Large, Ayrshire (Historic Scotland).

COFFINS

A solid plain wooden coffin would have been the norm for interments, the precursor of today's somewhat more ostentatious highly polished forms. It was a custom to place the simple wooden coffin inside a sealed lead outer coffin. This often carried heraldry and an inscription to identify the occupant. The armorial achievement was modelled and cast in lead and then fixed to the outer container with solder. Examples of armorial lead cases are to be found in the Skelmorlie Aisle, Largs, holding the remains of Sir Robert Montgomery and his wife.

FUNERAL PALLS

Another form of covering was used for the coffin during the funeral service; this was a piece of dark **cloth** with a **fringed** edge known as the funeral pall.

Heraldic funeral pall of John, 3rd Marquess of Bute, d. 1900, at Mount Stuart, Isle of Bute (Burnett).

Many kirks possessed a pall for use by poor parishioners which could be hired for a small fee but wealthy families retained their own pall, decorated with the appropriate heraldic devices. There is an

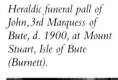

excellent heraldic pall in the private chapel of the Marquess of Bute at Mount Stuart which was made to cover the coffin of John, third Marquess of Bute, who died in 1900. This carries the arms of Crichton and Stuart and related families and has a decorative fringe in the livery colours of the family.

Craft and Trade Guilds in the burghs kept palls for their own guild members and these were embroidered with guild heraldry.

The use of an heraldic funeral pall is another practice which survives into the present day; a pall was recently made for the use of members of the Order of St John in Scotland which bears the heraldic white Maltese cross of the Order.

TOMBS

Depending on the wealth of the individual, an elaborate tomb would be raised above the last resting place, and once again heraldry was employed to identify the individual.

A tombstone carved with a mock heraldic device (Burnett).

Scotland's older burial grounds provide a wealth of armorial display which is often enhanced with the symbols of immortality – skulls, bones, hour-glasses, spades, mourning bells – and also with hopeful symbols of the Resurrection. If an individual was not armigerous then stonemasons produced pseudo-heraldic carvings with either initials on a shield shape, surmounted with helmet and mantling, or with symbols indicating how the dead person had made a living: a ship or anchor represented a sailor, scissors for a tailor, or the culter of a plough for a farmer.

Mention has already been made of **Greyfriars Cemetery** in Edinburgh which contains one of the best concentrations of funerary monuments reflecting both the varying wealth and status of those who found their final resting place. It offers a fine opportunity to view heraldic display in a funereal setting.

ENDPIECE

HERALDRY TODAY

THE LION REJOICES STILL

Symbolism in contemporary life is more prevalent than ever before. We are surrounded daily by logos, the fashionable substitute for written language which echo the pictographic quality of heraldic changes – a system of visual communication devised in an age of illiteracy. Public conveniences no longer bear *Gents* or *Ladies*, instead we have an image of a man and a woman. So, as we approach the millennium, civilisation comes full circle to an international system of signage echoing the medieval circumstances which gave rise to the science of heraldry.

OPPOSITE: Volumes from the Public Register of All Arms and Bearings in Scotland, commenced 1672 (Lyon Office).

Old usage still prevails for identification of property, on personal jewellery or public display. Heraldic bookplates ensure a borrowed book returns to its rightful owner. A crested letterhead identifies the sender. Signet rings or Highland wear accessories are engraved with crest or arms which also adorn personal jewellery of personal arms provides an inexpensive colourful method of decoration for many forms of occasion.

Bookplate of Ross Herald of Arms (Burnett).

Just as there was a revival of heraldic interest at the end of the 19th century, so the end of the 20th century has seen a similar revival. In an age of mass consumerism, the individual seeks **identity** by having a unique set of personal symbols gathered together in a coat of arms. In Scotland, England, Ireland, Canada, South Africa and Spain natives of the country, their descendants living elsewhere, and those possessing property in these countries can petition for a Grant of Arms from the respective heraldic authority.

This means that for Scotland, the **Lyon Office** is still a very busy

95

Letters Patent granting arms to William Ralph McClymont Adams, dated 27 July 1977 (Burnett).

place. To those who suspect there are only a limited number of arms, and those of ancient date and of great families, or that heraldry has relevance only for the antiquarian or archivist, it may come as a surprise that while there have been some 5,500 arms entered in the register from 1672 to 1900, there have been more than 7,000 registered since then, on average one every five days, day in day out, peace or war, since the turn of the century. Indeed, the pace is ever

increasing with petitions for grants and matriculations being issued now at the rate of nearly one every working day. The Lyon Office also maintains a register of officially recognised family tartans as these are naturally seen to be within the Lord Lyon's jurisdiction over 'all badges and cognisances whatsoever borne and used'.

The impaled arms of Mary Queen of Scots and her husband the King of France rendered in stained glass at the Scottish National Portrait Gallery, Edinburgh (Burnett).

Perhaps one of the main reasons for this continued popularity lies in the **colour of heraldry**. Compared to the classical or medieval periods we live in a grey age where so much of our architectural surroundings in Scotland appears only in monochrome. The sparkle of gold leaf, the richness of armorial tinctures and the flutter of an heraldic banner not only provides protection to carved stone panels but gives visual variety to the environment. Heraldry has survived, and still has relevance after eight centuries, because it has adapted to changing fashions and social *mores*. It fulfils basic human characteristics, individuality, artistic creativity and human vanity. Here in Scotland the science of heraldry has been regulated and cared for to such a degree that it is regarded as the purest form to be found in Europe. As such it is one of the vital facets which make Scotland's heritage different from those of other countries and is a distinction to be nurtured and safeguarded.

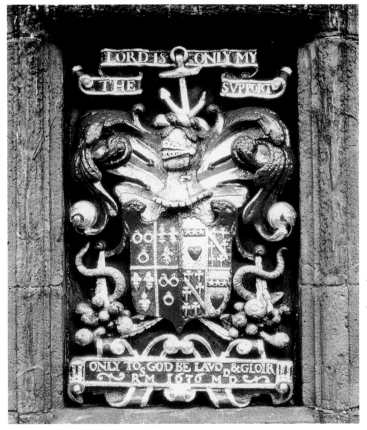

A fine example of exterior carved heraldry, painted with appropriate tinctures and gilded: the arms of Sir Robert Montgomerie of Skelmorlie (Historic Scotland). Worms eat the fruit and by analogy the dead, the panel giving in fine heraldic form what Gray portrays in his elegy: 'The boast of heraldry, the pomp of power, /And all that beauty, all that wealth e'er gave, /Awaits alike the inevitable hour. /The paths of glory lead but to the grave'.

GLOSSARY

Achievement: the complete pictorial display of arms comprising a shield, helmet, crest, *torse*, *mantling* and motto. If the *armiger* is entitled to them, *supporters*, additional mottoes or rallying cries, decorations and insignia of office may also be depicted.

Armiger: an individual who may lawfully bear arms.

Armigerous: personally entitled to ensigns armorial recognised in law.

Arms: the heritable right in a unique design of surface decoration for a shield, banner or other means of display and identification, composed in adherence with the rules of armory and duly and properly granted according to law by a competent heraldic authority, usually a sovereign or his depute. By extension, the whole such achievement.

Blazon: the conventional formula describing the design of arms or a whole achievement; also as a verb to make such a description.

Cadet: a junior member of a house; also an adjective: the family and heirs of a younger son form a *cadet* house.

Cadency: the status of being a *cadet* and the means whereby this noted in the cadet's armorial bearings.

Charge: an element placed upon a shield; as a verb it means to place upon: e.g. Gules a chevron Argent *charged* with three stars of the first (arms of Lord Jedburgh 1672).

Cognisances: the recognisable pattern, charges, or device which characterise the arms of a house.

Dexter: the right, and more honourable, side; in armory, however, this is determined from the perspective of one holding the shield. Thus the heraldic *dexter* side is the left as viewed.

Differencing: the practice of altering arms sufficiently to distinguish between members of the same house.

Entailed: tailzied, restricted by limitations on descent pursuant to terms of an original deed or grant, as to 'the heirs of the body of A' or 'next heirs male'.

Escutcheon: a shield, especially a small shield placed on top of a larger to display particularly significant arms.

Fief: a feu, a right in heritage held in feudal tenure by a vassal of his superior. Arms are themselves a feudal heritage.

Garb: a common *charge* representing a bound sheaf of corn.

Grant: of arms the formal assigning of ensigns armorial to a petitioner by Letters Patent under the seal of the Lyon Office in conjunction with their recordation in the Public Register of All Arms and Bearings.

Inescutcheon: a small shield shape used as a *charge*.

Lozenge: an acute diamond–shaped shield used to sport arms for females, in lieu of the customary shield shape, from the late Middle Ages until recent times; the oval cartouche is now preferred.

Mantling: the ornamental drapery falling down the back of a helmet in an armorial achievement; also called the *lambrequin* or *capeline.*

Marshalling: the systems and conventions of ordering multiple arms upon a single shield to denote marriage, descent, inheritance, honours or office.

Ordinaries: a selection of simple, bold geometric figures used in armory.

Patrilineal: relating to descent through the male line.

Sallet: a *salade* or form of helmet popular in the 15th century; rather like modern military helmets but with a narrow visor and an elongated tail projecting over the back of the neck.

Sinister: the heraldic left, that is, the viewer's right.

Supporters: the figures which may flank and 'support' a shield in the full achievement of one entitled to use them.

Tinctures: the conventional colours, metals, stains and furs recognised in armorial practice.

Torse: the conventionalised wreath of twisted silk in the dominant metal and colour of the arms which conceals the join of the crest and mantling to the helmet.

Totemism: the practice of identifying with a totem, an animal or object or symbol, which generates power, protection and identity.

INDEX

FURTHER READING

There is a wealth of very detailed volumes on all aspects of heraldry. We list here a few of the most recent and most readily available. These will all have bibliographies which will take the enthusiastic reader on more voyages of discovery.

Boutell, Charles, *Boutell's Heraldry*. First published as *The Manual of Heraldry* in 1863; revised by J P Brooke-Little and published by Warne, London, 1983.

Fox-Davies, Arthur Charles, *A Complete Guide to Heraldry*. Jack, London, 1909. Revised by J P Brooke-Little and published by Orbis, London, 1985.

Fox-Davies, Arthur Charles, *The Art of Heraldry*. Jack, London, 1904. Reprinted by Constable, London, 1981.

Friar, Stephen, ed., *A New Dictionary of Heraldry*. London, Black, 1987.

Innes of Learney, Sir Thomas, *Scots Heraldry*, 2nd edn. Edinburgh, Oliver & Boyd, 1956; this edition reprinted by Clearfield Company, Inc., Baltimore, 1994. Also revised by Sir Malcolm Innes of Edingight and printed by Johnston & Bacon, Edinburgh, 1978.

Moncrieffe of that Ilk, Sir Iain, Bt and Pottinger, J D H, *Simple Heraldry: Cheerfully Illustrated*. Edinburgh, Thomas Nelson, 1953. Revised and reprinted by Bartholomew, Edinburgh, 1978.

Urquhart, R M, *Scottish Civic Heraldry*. London, Heraldry Today, 1979.

Urquhart, R M, *Scottish Burgh and County Heraldry*. London, Heraldry Today, 1973.

Way of Plean, George and Squire, Romilly, *Scottish Clan and Family Enclyclopedia*. 1994.

The Heraldry Society of Scotland was founded in 1977 to further interest in and study of armoury in Scotland. Membership is open to all, and details may be obtained from: The Court of the Lord Lyon, New Register House, Edinburgh EH1 3YT.

SELECTIVE LIST OF SITES TO VISIT

ABERDEEN
Town House, Union Street
Mitchell Hall, Marischal College
St Machar's Cathedral, Old Aberdeen
Trinity Hall, Holburn Street

ABERDEENSHIRE
Crathes Castle (National Trust for Scotland)
Fyvie Castle (National Trust for Scotland)
Huntly Castle (Historic Scotland)
Muchalls Castle
Pitmedden Garden (National Trust for Scotland)
Tarves Kirkyard
Tolquhon Castle (Historic Scotland)
The Wine Tower, Fraserburgh

ANGUS
Edzell Castle, Edzell (Historic Scotland)
Glamis Castle, Glamis

ARGYLL
Luss Parish Kirk, Luss

BANFFSHIRE
Banff
Cullen Auld Kirk, Cullen
Deskford Kirk,
Duff House, Banff
Fordyce Kirkyard

DUMFRIES AND GALLOWAY
Caerlaverock Castle, Drumlanrig (Historic Scotland)
Lincludden Abbey (Historic Scotland)

DUNDEE
The Albert Institute, Customs House
Mercat Cross

EAST LOTHIAN
Pinkie House
Seton Collegiate Kirk (Historic Scotland)

EDINBURGH
The Castle (Historic Scotland)
Court of the Lord Lyon, New Register House
Greyfriars Kirkyard
The Palace of Holyroodhouse (Historic Scotland)
Royal Museum of Scotland
Scottish National Portrait Gallery
Thistle Chapel, St Giles High Kirk, High Street

FIFE
Culross
Falkland Palace (National Trust for Scotland)
Inverkeithing

GLASGOW
The Cathedral
The Highland Kirk
Kelvingrove Museum and Art Gallery
Provand's Lordship, High Street

INVERNESS
Chapel Yard, Railway Station
Town House

INVERNESS–SHIRE
Fort George (Historic Scotland)

MORAY
Elgin Cathedral (Historic Scotland)
Spynie Palace (Historic Scotland)

PERTHSHIRE
Weem Old Kirk

ROXBURGHSHIRE
Abbotsford House, Melrose
Queen Mary House, Jedburgh

WEST LOTHIAN
Linlithgow Palace (Historic Scotland)

Printed in Scotland for The Stationery Office Limited.   J12601, C30, 10/97, CCN 056901.